Fallen Sparrows

Other Books by Richard Shaw

Dagger John: The Life and Unquiet Times of Archbishop John Hughes of New York

The Christmas Mary Had Twins (originally published as *Elegy of Innocence*)

Pentecost Eve: Pondering Why the Holy Spirit Chose a Particular Time to Shake Us Awake with a Surprise Council

John Dubois: Founding Father

Chaplains to the Imprisoned: Sharing Life with the Incarcerated

Naked as a Jailbird

Fallen Sparrows

That One of These Little Ones Be Lost

Richard Shaw

RESOURCE *Publications* · Eugene, Oregon

Resource Publications
An Imprint of Wipf and Stock Publishers
199 W. 8th Ave., Suite 3
Eugene, OR 97401

www.wipfandstock.com

PAPERBACK ISBN: 978-1-6667-4794-2
HARDCOVER ISBN: 978-1-6667-4795-9
EBOOK ISBN: 978-1-6667-4796-6

01/25/23

For the past fifty-some years, I have been blessed to stand at the edge of the ministry of very many women and men who volunteer countless hours sharing life with the "residents" of jails and prisons. A local group of these in the Capital District of New York call their presence REC—"Residents Encounter Christ." They are the encounter with Christ.

I dedicate this book to their ministry.

And two of my siblings,
Edward Shaw and Regina Shaw Rohrwasser,
who did so much to make this book happen.

Contents

Preface

IN THE FIRST CHAPTER of this book, a Roman slave, Callistus, who has stolen from his master, is sentenced to work until death in mines, and a brand is burned into his forehead so that should he escape, the scar mark of the brand would always identify him as a criminal—even when in his later life he is much loved and raised to a unique historical role in the infant church. The scar on his forehead was his criminal "rap sheet."

The official term "rap sheet" grew during the Middle Ages, though etymologists aren't certain of what is meant by "rap." It might have been the act of someone being hit on the head or a judge pounding a gavel while saying, "Order in the court." The term now refers to a person's criminal history—e.g., "He has a rap sheet as long as his arm."

Public punishment is a public game of shame. This book tells the stories of criminals who had ever-growing rap sheets "as long as their arm." It also tells stories of men and women who reached out to help them move past this demeaning definition of self—to help these people who needed to hear and believe that they were loved by God.

I wrote this book because too many people tend to forget that this reality is at the very heart of the Christian message.

When I first began ministering in jails in the early 1970s, I was also teaching part-time in a Catholic high school. I once asked the students if they could bring in Christmas cards that could be given to the inmates so that they could send them to their families. I was somewhat taken aback to receive an indignant letter from the father of a tenth-grade student, hand delivered to me by his very embarrassed daughter. Her father told me that had I asked for cards for the victims of crime, he would gladly have let his daughter bring them in, but he was not about to subscribe to my catering to criminals.

I have since come to accept that a great proportion of Christians steadfastly vocalize an inflexible "lock 'em up and throw away the key" attitude about offenders. At mass, the "prayer of the faithful" oftentimes includes a petition: "For those who are unjustly imprisoned . . ." It would apparently be too jarring for those in the congregation to hear the flip side of this petition: "And for those who are justly imprisoned who nonetheless remain our sisters and brothers in the Lord . . ."

I have likewise come to expect that when public opinion polls are taken, a great number of Christians will endorse the death penalty. If the crime is heinous enough, sharp anger can be evoked by the suggestion that a criminal guilty of such a crime might have sought and received God's forgiveness before execution and, like Saint Dismas, be welcomed into heaven before the state-paid coroner has time to approach the executed corpse to officially pronounce death.

There is an overwhelming refusal to see convicted criminals as persons who are redeemable.

Yet, Christ, our eternal judge, tells us, "It is not the will of your heavenly Father that one of these little ones be lost. Are not two sparrows sold for a penny? Yet, not one of them will fall to the ground, apart from your Father . . . So do not be afraid: you are worth many sparrows" (Matt 10:26–29, 31; 18:14).

Chapter 1

The First Anti-Pope

THE WORD "CON" EVOKES more than one meaning. It can be used to describe a convict, someone doing time in prison. It can also refer to a confidence person, an individual with a winning personality who is an expert at gaining the confidence of others and then manipulating them to his/her own gain. Callistus, a "con" man in both senses—a Roman slave born in the latter part of the second century AD—would have been labeled a con artist regardless of what age he lived in. Given his activities in the particular setting of that era, he might easily remind one of Pseudolus, the wheeling and dealing slave who is the "hero" of both the comedy musical and the movie *A Funny Thing Happened on the Way to the Forum*.

Callistus's master was a man named Carpophorus, a Christian and an official member of the emperor's household. If it seems surprising that a Christian was in such a position, it must be remembered that after the first burst of persecution initiated by Nero, Rome had, with varying degrees of toleration, allowed Christianity to exist in its midst. This lasted until the third century, when belief in Christ and the growing strength of the church began to seriously rival that of belief in the officially honored state gods and state-run religion. Only then did the emperors embark on an all-out, last-ditch-stand persecution of Christians.

Nonetheless, during the intervening era of semi-tolerance, Christians were not liked by the majority of the Roman populace, who regarded them as an unpatriotic cult. In this atmosphere of prejudice, as noted by *The Cambridge Ancient History*, "Official action was taken against the Christians when special provocation so roused popular feeling that it resulted in definable charges against definite persons; granted that those who made accusations were sometimes raving mobs who with howls of execration at last dragged the mishandled victim of their frenzy before the tribunal."[1]

Property on the Move

The slave Callistus was a man who was quick to make the most of a profitable opportunity when he saw it. During the decade of the 180s, he persuaded his owner, Carpophorus, to establish a bank in the Piscina Publica, Rome's fish market. Callistus was ensconced as the bank's general manager and cashier, but the bank's credibility was based upon Carpophorus's good name. It was owing to this that many Christians, including a number of widows, deposited funds into the slave's care. Bad investments were made by the bank, and one day it was discovered that all the funds were gone. So was Callistus. Carpophorus was quickly informed that his property was among the missing and that his property that could move on two legs was hastily boarding a ship at a port on the Tiber River outside the city. He set out in pursuit and drew up at the port just in time to catch sight of his slave bank manager on a departing vessel.

Callistus, hearing his master's arresting yells, panicked and—in what one contemporary observer insisted was a suicide attempt—leaped overboard into the sea. When the ship's sailors dove in after him to save or capture him (depending upon one's interpretation of the events) he fought them off. Lifesaving methods finally prevailed, and Callistus was hauled back on board to be handed over to his owner.

1. Cook, *Imperial Crisis and Recovery*, 517.

Branded for Life

In court, Carpophorus contended that his slave was guilty of embezzlement. Callistus's only defense was that he had made a few bad investments. Whatever the case, the money was gone. Callistus was found guilty and sentenced to a special prison, the Pistrinum, for slaves convicted of crimes. The specific form of punishment exacted in the Pistrinum was the daily walking of a treadmill. A shocked eyewitness of this place wrote of the inmates:

> Ye gods, what men I saw there; their whole skin cut about with the lashes of the whip, and marked as if with paint; their gashed backs hung over with the tattered jackets rather than covered; some of them wore only a small girdle round their loins; in all of them their naked body could be seen through their rags. They were branded on their foreheads, their heads half shorn; on their feet they wore iron rings; their eyelids were as it were, eaten away by the vapor and smoke of the dark atmosphere, so that they scarcely had use of their eyes anymore.[2]

It is significant to keep in mind that Callistus, then, bore on his forehead, for the remainder of his life, his brand mark as an inmate of the Pistrinum. He was eventually paroled—not out of mercy but because bankrupted investors approached Carpophorus and argued that wheeling and dealing Callistus, having lost their money, was the only one who could track it down and regain it. Their only chance of his doing so was in his being on the streets instead of in prison.

On Parole

Given limited freedom, Callistus was placed in a seemingly hopeless situation. The contemporary observer who believed his dive into the Mediterranean was an attempt at suicide thought that—having nothing to pay and not being able to run away again on account of being watched—Callistus had devised a plan for his own destruction.

2. Dollinger, *Hippolytus and Callistus*, 616.

Seeking out his various business connections, Callistus had the temerity to pursue some of them, on a Sabbath, into a Jewish synagogue. Getting no satisfaction from confronting each of them individually as they entered, he followed them inside and berated them during the service. The congregation rose up and attacked him, beat him, and then dragged him through the streets to the court of Fuscianus, the prefect of the city. There, with some hyperbole, the whole crowd accused this single individual of starting a riot directed at them.

Callistus, in turn, tried his hand at hyperbole by claiming that the synagogue members were persecuting him because he was a Christian. His long-suffering master, who arrived at court at this point, debunked any claims that this felonious slave might make to being a brother of his in Christ.

Dead Man Walking in Sardinia

If Callistus had sought an occasion of death, the synagogue members were bent on helping him to it. They vehemently clamored that he be executed. In response, the prefect had him flogged and then ordered him to be sent to the mines of Sardinia. The sentence was intended to be a capital punishment. Sardinia was commonly known as "the island of death."

At the court of the reigning emperor, Commodus, was a Christian eunuch named Hyacinthus. In spite of his mutilation, he was respected by his fellow believers well enough to have been called to the presbyterate. The priest had raised an adopted daughter named Marcia, who, despite her religion, had become the mistress of the emperor.

Roman law, locked into a centuries-old caste system, forbade marriages between those of noble birth and those of lowborn birth. Nonetheless, despite the lack of official status, she was all-powerful with Commodus, having all the honors of an empress.

In the year 186 AD, Marcia sought to ease the sufferings of Christians who had been sent to Sardinia for no other reason than the prejudices of Roman citizens. She sent for Victor, bishop of the

Christians in Rome, and asked him for names of such individuals. At a moment which includes several "firsts" of history, this incident marks the first time that a pope is known to have had dealings with the imperial court of Rome. Victor drew up the requested list and in doing so purposely omitted Callistus, who had been sentenced to the mines not because of faith but for real criminal activity.

Hyacynthus, bearing the emperor's official pardons, arrived at the mines of Sardinia to proclaim release to the captives. As the Christians were being released, Callistus made the most of the opportunity. He threw himself at the feet of Hyacynthus, weeping profusely and begging to be included as a fellow member of the faith.

Moved with pity, the presbyter used his official power as a representative of the emperor and extended the pardon to include the embezzler and riot provoker whose name had intentionally been excluded.

Accepting a Papal Payoff

Rome did not build another triumphal arch to welcome the return of Callistus, who was now doubly free—for ownership of a slave convicted of crimes was transferred from his master to the state, and the state had chosen to free Callistus. Pope Victor hoped to avoid embarrassment for himself as the one who had drawn up the list of those to be pardoned, and to avoid embarrassment for the church, which was still suspect in the eyes of so many citizens. He struck a deal with Callistus. If the onetime slave would just disappear from view and move to the seaside town of Antium (present-day Anzio—site of one of the bloodiest battles of World War II), then he, Victor, would supply him with a monthly income. For an opportunist just released from prison, it was an offer he couldn't refuse.

Deacon Callistus

When Pope Victor died in 197 AD, a presbyter named Zephyrinus succeeded him as bishop of Rome. Whatever the previous connection was between Callistus and Zephyrinus, it is unknown to history. But shortly thereafter, Callistus resurfaced in Rome, and for the next twenty years, he was constantly at the pope's side, serving as his adviser and, more significantly, as his spokesman. He was ordained a deacon and placed in charge of the clergy of Rome. He was also given charge of a cemetery newly acquired by the Christian community. The acquirement of this place of burial, which—even today—is still called the "Cemetery of Callistus," marked another historical first. Prior to this, Christians had been buried in the private cemeteries of wealthy Christian families (still honored today as the celebrated "catacombs" of the days of persecution). This purchase of land for a "Christian cemetery" is the first known instance of the church acquiring land owned in its own name. It was a great step forward in the church becoming publicly established.

The management of this cemetery, along with his supervision of the city's presbyters, placed Callistus in a position which, in the judgment of *The Oxford Dictionary of Popes*, "made him the real power in the Roman Church."[3]

The First and Foremost Presbyter

Enter Hippolytus. He was a Roman priest and, more significantly, a voluminous writer and theologian. Jean Danielou, a modern theologian and historian, described him "first and foremost as a representative of the old Roman presbyterate, whose catechetical tradition and liturgical usages he retains." The historian felt compelled to add, however, that Hippolytus, unfortunately, had "a reactionary spirit."[4]

He was important enough a man that his contemporary adherents had commissioned a statue made of him—seated, seemingly enthroned. Lost for centuries, the statue was unearthed in 1551 AD and placed in the Vatican library. Its identification was

3. Kelly, *Oxford Dictionary*, 15.

4. Danielou, *Christian Centuries*, 150.

easy, for the sculptor had carved a partial list of Hippolytus's literary contributions on the back of the chair. These works included a complicated calculation of how to figure out when to celebrate Easter and a work which preserved for history the church's most ancient, complete eucharistic prayer—a prayer which would contribute to a modern-day irony. After the Second Vatican Council, some—Catholics who were, like Hippolytus, inclined to a "reactionary spirit"—resented the addition of "new" eucharistic prayers.

One of these, "Eucharistic Prayer II," was the ancient canon of Hippolytus. He also wrote a work, *Summary against the Heresies*, in which, as judged by the *Catholic Encyclopedia*, "his vehemence, intransigence and rigorousness led him to make attacks on strictly orthodox positions, theology, Church organization and discipline."[5]

Hippolytus voiced shock that Pope Zephyrinus allowed Callistus, bearing the brand mark of a convict, to be always with him. He attacked the two on dogmatic grounds—for teaching heresy about the Trinity. The present-day Christian who might (or might not) be able to mouth a definition of the Trinity learned from a childhood catechism must accept the fact that Jesus, in revealing God as "Triune," gave us the merest glimpse of that which is infinitely beyond the grasp of the human mind. There is no facile biblical explanation of the nature of God. The apostles, at the church's first general Council of Jerusalem (Acts 15), never addressed the question. They were more concerned with concrete, practical problems such as whether gentiles had to be circumcised and follow Jewish ritual customs.

For the next two and a half centuries, the fathers of the Christian community fought and hammered away at definitions and readily flung the word "heretic" at any opponent who disagreed with their own school of thought. It must be kept in mind that Callistus and Hippolytus lived a full century short of the time of the Council of Nicaea, where a creed statement was finally promulgated about the Trinity. They lived in an age which was hacking its way through theological verbiage in search of a definition. Callistus,

5. McGuire, "St. Hyppolytus of Rome."

who—according to Hippolytus—led Zephyrinus into heresy, leaned toward the thinking of a theological writer named Sabellius.

The teaching of this school of thought, eventually labeled Patripassianism, taught that the Father and Son were so much one that when the Son suffered and died on the cross, the Father did as well. Hippolytus rejected this and clearly separated the persons of the Father and Son, doing so with such emphasis that Callistus accused him of teaching that there were, in effect, two Gods.

What really bothered Hippolytus was that this was not just a theological dispute on paper. Con artists have to be attractive people; if they are not, they could never earn such an appellation for themselves, and Callistus had most certainly shown an ability to win the confidence of those who knew him personally. Hippolytus accused his adversary of being a demagogue who played to all theological parties and swayed them to himself.

In the Shoes of the Fisherman

In 217 AD, Pope Zephyrinus died, and to the horror of Hippolytus, the Christian community of Rome proclaimed the popular Callistus as their bishop. The wheeling and dealing, onetime slave, the embezzling, convicted criminal and ex-jailbird with a rap sheet as long as his arm, was now Pope Callistus I.

Hippolytus, so theologically prestigious, so morally upright, had every right to see himself as the perfect candidate for this office. In much the same way there must have been at least one potential pope who, in 1958 AD sat in the Conclave, stunned to see the unlikely election of John XXIII, the broadly smiling, affable peasant who others presumed would at most be a brief interim pope. In a scant five years time John thrust the church forward into a new consciousness of self and of mission to the world. Serving as pope for the exact same amount of time, Callistus did much the same for the church of the third century.

In the quest for the proper dogmatic statement of the nature of the Trinity, he bowed, showing no little amount of humility, to the doctrinal formulation of the expert theologian Hippolytus, and condemned the doctrine of Patripassianism as taught by Sabellius. In responding to the proclamation of this, Hippolytus, as a priest, showed that, at that moment of time, he technically accepted the authority of Callistus, both as his own bishop and as the unifying bishop of the universal church.

Nonetheless, instead of accepting the tribute paid to himself by the new pope, he claimed it as a victory of the stronger man over the weaker, much as Paul had once crowed about flying into Peter's face and bending Peter's authoritative will to his own. Hippolytus insisted that it was through fear of him as a theologian that the new pope had bowed to him.

If Callistus was willing to concede points in the mysterious realm of dogmatic theology, he nonetheless boldly launched into the realms of moral theology to move the church into a deeper realization of its Christian mission in society. Throughout the centuries, each generation of believers has had to balance Christ's call to be a holy community and his call to embrace sinners. Are Christians, born again in faith, to be a puritan community, a citadel of perfection, a people called apart; or, in contrast to this, is it to be a community which, receiving Christ's forgiveness, becomes an instrument of continual forgiveness to others?

Initially, the dogmatically strict Hippolytus would choose the former, but with time and circumstance, he would choose the latter.

Callistus, the onetime criminal who had lived in such a sinful world, espoused the idea of a church of mercy. In his teaching the church was not merely to embrace former sinners but was to embrace continually falling sinners within the community; the confession of sins made by the congregation at the beginning of each liturgy was to reflect a reality. With this in mind he promulgated policies that were as radical to the third century as the policies of John XXIII would seem to the mid-twentieth century.

If persecution of the church was sporadic, it nevertheless presented a constant thread in the lives of the faithful, and not all of them were born to be heroes. Nor were they all born to be great theologians. Many believers drifted in and then out of the community either because apostasy meant safety or because they were confused by the theologies eventually branded as heresy (or orthodoxy) taught by such groups as the Arians, Manichaeiests, and the followers of such men as Sabellius.

Callistus taught that the Christian sign of penance had to be real; that apostates, heretics, and the great mass of everyday sinful people could be brought back into a Christian community from which they had turned away. Even within this attitude, a great deal of latitude could be chosen. As Karl Baus observes in "From the Apostolic Community to Constantine": "Even if convinced in principle that a second penance was not to be refused to such sinners, it was possible in the practice of penitential discipline to choose stricter or milder forms according to whether emphasis was placed on the Christian ideal of holiness or on the Christian teachings of mercy."[6]

Callistus chose the extreme of mercy and flung open the doors to all. He not only readmitted those who had fallen away, he permitted priests and bishops to remain in office even if they had been guilty of grave sin. He allowed men to be ordained to the priesthood who had been married more than once, and, against the growing custom of celibacy in the Western territory of the church, declared that if a priest married after receiving orders, he was not guilty of sin in doing so.

He issued one church law which flew directly in the face of Roman civil law. Marcia, the concubine of the emperor, who had freed Christian prisoners and in doing so had freed the criminal Christian Callistus, had been forbidden by Rome's law to marry the emperor. Callistus, as religious leader of the Christian community, defied this law and allowed such marriages, even sanctioning marriages between free women and slaves.

6. Baus, "From the Apostolic Community," 24.

Pope for an "Elect Community of Pure Souls"

This was the straw which broke the camel's back of Hippolytus's growing resistance to the authority of Callistus. As noted by the historian Louis Duchesne in his *Early History of the Christian Church: From Its Foundation to the End of the Fifth Century*, "Hippolytus had never been conspicuous for mildness, but between [the issuing of his works] the *Syntagma* and the *Labyrinth* his character had embittered considerably. The mere mention of Callistus makes him furious."[7]

Irrationally, he fought against his religious superior by stretching logic into illogic. He projected that if the church allowed free women to marry slaves when such marriages were not allowed by the civil government, the children of these unions would be considered base born and women would commit abortions to prevent such births. Laying the guilt of such a possibility squarely upon Callistus, Hippolytus declared that he was teaching fornication and murder at the same time.

The great popularity of Callistus among a populace that understood human frailty only too well is not surprising. Yet, Hippolytus expressed amazement that this bishop drew so many along with him. With increasing vehemence he began to label him a juggler and an impostor. He had become so convinced that Callistus, as bishop of Rome, was in error, he began to style himself as the proper leader of the true church. Most likely neither he nor his followers would ever have coined the term "anti-pope" as historians would eventually use it. Their only consideration was that Hippolytus was "orthodox" while Callistus was not, and that the followers of Hippolytus, removed and apart from the common rabble of unworthy Christians were an elect community of pure souls sharply and uncompromisingly separated from the world and its dangers.

Hippolytus took to referring to the church from which he had separated only as "the 'school' of Callistus" as if it were a group of secular philosophers. Given his own acknowledged prestige as a

7. Duchesne, *Early History*, 288.

great historian, his stance might have carried more weight if he had taken it at the time of Callistus's election. As it was he had waited until Callistus had become firmly established as an authority (an authority acknowledged as valid by Hippolytus in the matter of dealing with Sabellius). Also, he made his move after Callistus had set forth compassionate policies that responded to urgent needs of Christians living in the capital of a pagan empire.

In a public reaction that must have surprised the self-assured Hippolytus, very few people outside of his own immediate "school" followed after him, and his schism caused very little stir in the universal church. As the historian Jean Danielou judged, Hippolytus and his followers may have "dreamed of a Church which was a handful of saints in conflict with the world . . . but the pastors who had charge of souls could not accept this vision."[8]

Ex-Convict, Martyr, and Saint

In the year 222 AD during an anti-Christian riot Callistus was killed in the Trastevere section of Rome. History has no details concerning the exact circumstances of his death. Thus one might wonder at first reaction if the onetime riot provoker and criminal had gotten himself into a battle reflective of his early career. What we do know belies this. Most importantly, Hippolytus, who continued writing with venom about Callistus and his "school," says nothing of the manner of his death. Considering the fact that he continued to republish the facts of his early career in crime, he would have pounced upon any ignoble circumstances of his violent demise. But he avoids mentioning this. If he cannot say anything bad, he will say nothing at all.

From the time of his death onward Callistus was venerated as a martyr and saint by the community that saw him die. Frescoes decorating his tomb portray his martyrdom as heroic and not an accidental occurrence. And although the cemetery that he had managed as a deacon was thereafter named after him and became

8. Duchesne, *Early History*, 228.

the burial place of the popes, beginning with his successor, he was buried in the vicinity of his martyrdom and a Basilica (Santa Maria in Trastevere) was built within the next century as a shrine in his honor. The beloved and compassionate jailbird pope had been immediately canonized by the people of Rome.

Remaining Self-Deluded

Hippolytus's claim to be the true bishop of Rome, by merit of his intelligence and righteousness, was largely ignored. The community elected Urban I as Callistus's successor. Thoroughly embittered, the prolific Hippolytus wrote of his dead adversary's disciples, that being pleased with his doctrines crowds continued to flock to his "school." This crowded rabble of a "school" continued to be guilty of not making any distinctions as to who is worthy to be in their community, offering communion to all in a "catholic" ("all gathering") "assembly of faith" ("ecclesia"—"church.")

When Urban died in 230 AD, Pontian was elected to succeed him. Entrenched with his handful of followers, Hippolytus battled on, crying out his claim to leadership to all who would listen. Throughout this period of time Rome had been ruled by emperors who were at least passively tolerant of Christianity. When persecutions erupted such as that which caused the martyrdom of Callistus, they were generally mob-provoked by citizens who considered their violence to be patriotic and gods-fearing. In 235 AD a onetime officer of the guards, Maximus Thrax, became emperor and actively persecuted leaders of the Christian community. He arrested Pontian, the acknowledged bishop of Rome, and Hippolytus, who claimed to be bishop of Rome, condemning both of them to the mines of Sardinia.

The nineteenth-century historian John von Dollinger offers an interesting theory: that the arrest of the two rival bishops may have been caused not by direct persecution of the Christians, but as a reaction to the disturbance of the peace created by the religious dispute, much the same as the banishment of the Jews from the city by the emperor Claudius in the first century AD was owing to their internal dispute over an unnamed Jew referred to as "Chrestus." ("the anointed one").

Whatever the cause of the arrests, Hippolytus ironically found himself cast into the same prison mine as the onetime target of his criticism, the jailbird Callistus. The irony is all the greater if it is true that the arrest resulted not from religious persecution but from a charge of disturbing the peace. And yet, this moment of shame became a moment of grace.

Peace and Healing on Death Row

The first general persecution of Christianity under Nero had been a reaction to a new and peculiar sect. In the third century, with leaders such as Callistus who promulgated marriage laws which wiped away the empire's caste system, the church, growing yearly in size and strength, was clearly on a collision course with the civil government of Rome. In the latter part of this century, the empire struck back in a last ditch attempt to destroy what was becoming a rival authority.

Pontian, in the prison mine of Sardinia, became the first pope to resign from office, doing so on September 28, 255 (which, listed in a fourth-century record book, stands as the first precisely recorded date in the history of the papacy). His impending martyrdom was inescapable. His resignation allowed for an immediate continuity of authority in the church at a time when a sign of authority was so essential.

And then, Hippolytus came to his senses as a Christian. Sharing imprisonment with Pontian, he made peace with him. The "school of Callistus" which he had once claimed had wrongfully called itself "a catholic church" was the Catholic Church. His act of heroic self-humiliation and peace left no cause for his own school to elect a successor to continue the schism. History's first antipope went to his martyrdom along with the pope whom history has placed in the line of successors to Saint Peter.

It was a lesson in forgiveness for both factions. Both had to bend, both had to become one in reconciliation. The church of

Rome brought back the bodies of the two martyrs and buried them on the same day. The anti-pope Hippolytus has been, for his greatness of soul at the end of his life, canonized as Saint Hippolytus, and his feast day each year is celebrated on the same day as the pope with whom he shared martyrdom, Saint Pontian.

The lesson is a warning that, whenever we are tempted to follow the initial pathway of the righteous and rigorous Hippolytus, who would have stigmatized a onetime criminal to remain in the eyes of all a lifelong criminal, we are moving away from the teachings of Christ and his church.

Chapter 2

The Overly Forgiven

IN MAY OF 1970, when Alessandro Serenelli died at the age of eighty-eight, *The New York Times* recorded his passing, as did *Newsweek* and other major international publications.[1] His name, included that year in the published *Guide to Periodical Literature*,[2] is followed by the words "Italian Murderer," as if this were a generic category of listing. His single act of killing, which had occurred during an attempted rape, happened sixty-eight years earlier, in July of 1902. The immediate and inflamed public reaction to his crime, and the subsequent veneration of his victim, has placed the incident in history as one of the most well-known single acts of violence of the entire twentieth century.[3]

1. One can see the total page of *The New York Times* story of Serenelli on the internet.

2. *Readers' Guide to Periodical Literature.*

3. There are many accounts of the murder of Saint Maria Goretti, and she is one of the most popular saints of the twentieth century. While her murderer, Alessandro Serenelli was still alive, living in a monastery, esteemed author Pietro di Donato spent many days interviewing him. He wrote a definitive account, *The Penitent.* It was my main resource in writing this chapter. See "Alessandro Serenelli" on Wikipedia.

Trapping His Victim

At the time of the crime's occurrence, Alessandro was twenty years of age and had long since left boyhood behind. He had spent five years at sea and two years after that as a farm laborer. It might be said that his eleven-year-old victim, Maria Goretti, had also grown beyond childhood. Her mother Assunta had been widowed with six small children, of whom Maria was the third oldest. Assunta and those of her brood who were old enough worked as tenant farmers in Ferriere, a small village south of Rome, on land shared with Giovanni Serenelli and his son. Maria labored as an adult and with her mother raised the younger children.

On the morning of the murder, Alessandro, who had made several bumbling and unsuccessful attempts to attract the attentions of Maria, gruffly asked her to mend a shirt for him. At midday she was sitting on the stairway outside the house shared by both families, minding her infant sister Therese and mending the shirt when Alessandro returned from the fields and pushed past her, climbing the stairs to the second story kitchen. He called to her to come to him. She did so without suspicion or question. As she entered the door, he grabbed her and pulled her to him, attempting to force himself upon her. She reacted immediately and as forcefully as she could. Telling him that he was committing a sin she struggled and screamed for her mother. Alessandro had taken a brush hook from a tool box as he came to the house and had stuck it under his belt. He pulled out the hook and stabbed her fourteen times. Leaving her mortally wounded on the floor, he hid in his room as family members came to the house, responding to her cries for help.

In the immediate panic of discovery the only concern was for Maria. She was taken by ambulance to a hospital. There was little the doctors could do. Many of the stabs had pierced vital organs. She lived into the next day, remaining conscious. She received Holy Communion, and told the priest:

"I forgive Alessandro and want him to be with me in Paradise." And then she died.

To Forgive as Does Christ

The story of her heroic defense of virtue and the innocence with which she forgave her murderer inflamed the territory. On the day of her funeral in nearby Netunno, shops were closed as if for a sacred occasion and thousands attempted to push into the church. They did not share in Maria's act of forgiveness. A collective rage was directed toward Alessandro. On the day of the attack the police had pulled him from the farmhouse, tied him by rope to a saddle, and dragged him, barefoot, walking behind the horse, to the local jail. Fear of mob justice impelled the authorities to move him to Rome's Regina Coeli prison.

It was from there, three months later, that he was taken to trial. In the crowded courtroom he refused to let his defense lawyer put forth any mitigating circumstances to help save himself. He testified that "Maria Goretti did not lend cause to my desire or lead me on in any way."

When the presiding judge asked Maria's mother if she had anything to say, Assunta shocked the packed court room by saying:

"Yes, sir, Mr. President. I forgive Alessandro."

An uproar ensued. Calmly, Assunta turned to the angry crowd and asserted:

"And suppose, in turn, Jesus Christ does not forgive us."

The court sentenced Alessandro to thirty years of hard labor, the first three of which were to be spent in solitary confinement. He spent these next three years alone in a closed, four-walled cell, his first assigned labor the gluing together of matchbooks, his second, after a move to a prison in Noto, Sicily, the separating of palm leaf fibers for the production of rope. In October of 1905 he emerged from solitary confinement to take his place with other prisoners working a wheel to turn fibers into cord. Even in population he remained solitary, bitterly living within his own mind.

The Dream

Two years after this, as he later related, he had a dream in which he saw Maria coming toward him with lilies. She gave them to him one by one, and as she did the flowers turned into beams of light. She then promised him that he would one day be in heaven with her.[4]

Not long after this he received a visit from Bishop Giovanni Blandini of Noto. The gentle concern of the bishop helped to awaken Alessandro to a sense of spirituality. He began to be a regular at Mass. He asked the chaplain for books and became a student of his own faith.

World War I did not touch his existence except that he was moved to a prison in Siracusa where he worked on a gang transporting stone to a seaport. His only contact with the outer world was his sister-in-law Maria, who corresponded with him regularly. In 1918 she wrote that Alessandro's father had died in a poorhouse. He had been emotionally destroyed by the murder and had borne on the streets the guilt his son bore in prison. For the remainder of Alessandro's life the effect which his crime had upon his father would weigh heavily upon his heart.

After the war he was transferred to the prison colony of Bitti in Sardinia. The colony, set upon a plateau three thousand feet above the sea, was run as a farm. Returned to work on the soil Alessandro spent the decade of the 1920s living a self-imposed monastic spiritual life. He remained a loner, sharing only limited friendships among his fellow convicts.

In 1929 the prince of Piedmont, as a gesture on his wedding day, granted amnesty to some long-term prisoners with exemplary records. Alessandro, having served twenty-seven years of his thirty-year sentence, was on the list of those to be freed.

He was returned to Regina Coeli prison in Rome and then transported south by train to Torrette for his release. The public ordinarily has a short memory. Most long-term convicts return to

---

4. In 1961 he wrote a public letter that can be found online. In it he wrote, "Little Maria was my light, my protectress. I served those 27 years in prison well."

society as forgotten people. The very opposite was so with Alessandro. Devotion to his victim, Maria, had grown over the generation and a half he had spent in prison. She had become a model of heroic purity throughout the world, and there was a strong move toward her canonization as a saint.

Pope Pius X, as early as 1908, had spoken of her in his sermon on the feast of the Immaculate Conception, calling her "the Saint Agnes of the twentieth century."[5]

The Coming Forth of Lazarus

On the train bound for Torretti the guard who was transferring him for release passed to Alessandro a newspaper article which began, "Today the killer of Maria Goretti has completed his debt to society." The guard said:

"As a boy I read of your crime. My wife and daughters are devoted to the Goretti girl. And here I am taking you to freedom and your hometown. The strangeness of life." As is a prison guard and a prisoner sharing this reality together.

Alessandro studied the article, finding it "a weave of fact and fiction."[6] He was described as a sex mad beast; his father as a heartless drunkard. As he was set free he was advised:

"You will be expected to walk the edge of the razor. If I were you I would migrate and change my identity."

Alessandro agreed with the assessment.

"I return as a Lazarus," he said, "who wishes to be forgotten."

He chose not to migrate, though his adolescence at sea had given him the experience of travel. At forty-seven years of age he decided to stay near his home, even though all of his social contacts had ended the hour of Maria's death. He became a migrant

5. Saint Agnes lived in the fourth-century Roman Empire. She was thirteen years of age when a local governor brought her to his house to make her his sexual victim. She held him off and as punishment he placed her in a house of prostitution. When she still maintained her chastity he had her beheaded. Delaney, *Dictionary*, 32.

6. Di Donato, *Penitent*, 130–31.

farm worker, and even though his brother arranged for him a marriage with a widow's daughter, he decided not to accept. He feared the stigma of his crime passing on to any children he might beget.

He also feared to make any contact with Maria's family. Assunta Goretti lived in the nearby town of Corinaldo, working in a parish rectory. He never went near the place. As Christmas of 1934 approached, the parish priest in Corinaldo, Don Frencesco Bernacchio, took the initiative. He wrote to Alessandro, invited him to come for the holidays, and enclosed train fare.

On Christmas Eve Assunta answered the rectory door. Alessandro stood before her. It had been thirty-one years since they had seen one another at his trial. He asked her:

"Do you recognize me?"

"Yes, my son," she said.

He crumbled to his knees and blurted words that had been pent up within him for decades:

"Do you forgive me, Assunta? Dear Assunta, forgive me, forgive what I have done to Maria and you."

She gently caressed his head.

"Alessandro," she said, "Marietta forgave you. Christ has forgiven you, and why should not I also forgive? I forgive you, of course, my son."

She had only one reproach for him. As he stood up she said:

"Why haven't I seen you before this? You are a long-suffering son to me."[7]

Two of Assunta's sons had emigrated to America. The infant Therese, whom Maria had been minding the day of the murder, was now a nun. Another daughter, Ersilia, lived near her mother, raising her own family. On this Christmas Eve Assunta brought Alessandro to Ersilia's home for dinner.

Then, as a family, they went to midnight Mass, where the people of Corinaldo witnessed Assunta kneeling next to Alessandro to receive Communion.

---

7. Di Donato, *Penitent*, 141–42. On the internet there is a large photo of Assunta and Alessandro, sitting next to one another, many years later, love written in their expressions.

After this public act of love, there was no excuse for anyone to treat Alessandro as an outcast. And yet he continued to live as such, moving about and performing transient work as a farm hand. Again, Don Bernacchio intervened, arranging for a position for him at a Capuchin monastery at Anondola.

The Vulnerability of an Ex-Convict

Shortly after Alessandro began work there, an elderly monastery servant named Mugnetto raised the cry that his hidden life savings had been stolen, some four thousand lire. The police were called, and when they arrived, a scenario was played out which every ex-convict must always fear. Alessandro Serenelli was a man with a criminal record; therefore, he was immediately assumed to be the culprit. He was arrested and put in jail, where he remained for fifteen days until it was discovered that Mugnetto had made a false accusation. There had been no theft. The old man had feared that Serenelli would take his own job if he stayed at the monastery and had trumped up the accusation in order to be rid of him.

Alessandro was freed, but the Capuchins at that particular monastery, acting as if the accusation itself were enough to make him unfit as an employee, advised him not to come back to them. Returning to Corinaldo to resume working as a migrant field hand, he again experienced Don Bernacchio being Barnabas to his being Saul. The priest arranged for him to work at another Capuchin monastery, this one in Ascoli Picenco. He was fifty-four years of age when he entered the employ of these friars. He remained with them for the rest of his life. In his 1961 public letter, he wrote, "The Brothers of St. Francis, Capuchins from Marche, welcomed me with angelic charity into their monastery as a brother, not as a servant. I've been living with their community for 24 years."[8]

World War II devastated this area of Italy. The Benedictine Monastery of Monte Cassino, which had seen more than a millennium of history, was reduced to rubble by Allied bombings. Anzio,

8. "Alessandro Serenelli Letter," para. 9.

a handful of miles from Netunno, was the site of the beachhead for the invading American forces.

Netunno subsequently provided a shrine site not only for the body of Maria Goretti but for the thousands of American soldiers who died in the invasion and whose final resting place is in the American military cemetery at the edge of this small village.

It was after the war that the cause for Maria's canonization moved forward to its fulfillment. In 1947 a film entitled *Over the Marshes* was released, telling the story of her martyrdom at the hands of Alessandro Serenelli. His identity unknown to those around him, he sat in a theater and watched the story unfold as concocted in the imaginations of filmmakers. He later said that the movie was "a disservice to the truth. I do not talk about their portrayal of myself, whom they twisted in a thousand ways, but they put my father in a dark light. He did not deserve that."[9]

In that same year, Maria was beatified by Pope Pius XII. Of this occasion, Alessandro wrote: "While here in the Monastery of Ascoli Picenco I read that I was in Rome. They said I was especially invited to Maria's beatification and was there in the Vatican and Saint Peter's wearing sacerdotal robes and with the long Capuchin beard, all inventions of newspaper fantasy! But it is not important what they say about me, and perhaps their fanciful exaggerations constitute part of the expiation for me of the awful crime I blindly committed as a youth."[10]

On June 24, 1950, Pius canonized Saint Maria Goretti in a ceremony which drew such a vast popular response that it had to be moved from within Saint Peter's to the square outside, the first time this had been done with a canonization ceremony. It was also the first time in history that the mother of a saint was present for such a ceremony. Assunta had been crippled by a stroke in 1944, the year of the military battles that had been fought around Netunno. She lived for another four years after her daughter was declared a saint.

9. Di Donato, *Penitent*, 185–86.

10. Di Donato, *Penitent*, 159.

In October of 1954 she became very ill. Her surviving children, who considered Alessandro one of the family, sent for him. It added greatly to his grief that, although he traveled as quickly as he could, he didn't arrive before she died.

He lived for almost another full generation of time. He was famous, and because it was now a pious thing for pilgrims to do, they wanted to bathe him, drown him in their own pieties. The monastery at Ascoli Picenco had become a tour stop. The friars, who now cared for Alessandro as if he had taken full vows, moved the aged man to their monastery at Macerata, which was less accessible to the merely curious.

In the early 1960s one pilgrim did gain access to him, only after first winning the confidence of the friars, and then the reluctant confidence of the octogenarian Alessandro, who now lived his days intent on prayer. Pietro Di Donato, an American author, gently drew Alessandro into conversation that was at first hesitant. From his interviews he wrote a restrained and beautiful book-length study of Alessandro, *The Penitent*. It is the portrait of a soul who is as worthy a candidate of canonization as was his victim. A decade later, when at last God called him from this life, *The New York Times* judged Alessandro important enough a historical figure to be given an obituary. The *Times* quoted him, calmly remembering the promise given to him in a vision while he was in prison.

"I know that Maria will welcome me to heaven when my time comes," he said, "She has forgiven me."

Chapter 3

Inmate Mindszenty

Comrade in Misery

IN THE DEBRIS AND confusion following World War II, Soviet-dominated communist regimes consolidated power throughout Eastern Europe. Any opposition to this new Eastern Bloc monolith was quashed, and this included opposition from the church. In Hungary in 1948, the country's cardinal primate, Jozsef Mindszenty, fought against the government's nationalization of Catholic schools. He was arrested, imprisoned, and tortured both mentally and physically. During one interrogation session he was stripped naked and made to stand in the center of a large room. In his own words:

> The tormentor raged, roared, and in response to my silence took the implements of torture into his hands. This time he held the truncheon in one hand, a long sharp knife in the other. And then he drove me like a horse in training, forcing me to trot and gallop. The truncheon lashed down on my back repeatedly for sometime without a pause. Then he stood still and brutally threatened: "I'll kill you; by morning I'll tear you to pieces and throw the remains of your corpse to the dogs or into the canal. We are the masters now." Then he forced me to begin running again. Although I was gasping for breath and

the splinters of the wooden floor stabbed painfully into
my bare feet, I ran as fast as I could to escape his blows.[1]

In February of 1949, at a show trial, the forced confessions
of the gaunt, hollow-eyed prisoner were presented, along with the
state's trumped up evidences of treason. Found guilty, the cardinal
was sentenced to life imprisonment. Kept in solitary confinement
in a closed, closet-like cell, Mindszenty craved the companion-
ship not of the guards whom he could occasionally see, but of his
unseen fellow inmates who suffered as he did. One day as he was
being returned from a walk in the exercise yard the guard accidentally opened the door not to Mindszenty's cell but to the cell
next to it. He ordered the prisoner to enter. Mindszenty noticed
the mistake at once, and later reflected that he had never before so
willingly obeyed an order. It was a hot day. The cell's occupant lay
undressed on his cot. Startled, he reacted not to the presence of the
guard but to his previously unseen neighbor.

The two convicts looked, probing into each other's eyes, and
although afterward the horrified guard wrenched him back out
into the corridor, Mindszenty consoled the officer for his dangerous mistake and promised silence of the matter. He later reflected
that he actually was grateful to him for this single opportunity to
see a comrade in misery. Later that night, Mindszenty tapped on
the wall and received an answering tap. This began a communication which lasted for months; two human beings able to show their
compassion for one another.

Abruptly, one day, the response of his neighbor stopped.
Mindzsenty wondered whether the man had decided to obey the
prison regulation forbidding such communication, or had been
released, or taken sick, or even died. He spent an entire sleepless
night worrying about the matter. Shortly afterwards some small
repair was carried out in his cell, and for a little while he was put in
the empty neighboring cell. He stayed there a few hours, sat at his
table, lay on his bed, thought about him, and tried to imagine who
he might have been.

1. Mindszenty, *Memoirs*, 172.

Cardinal Mindszenty was jailed because of his religious faith. He was aware of the possibility that the fellow inmate with whom he had shared "compassion" was a justly-convicted criminal guilty of serious crime. It made him realize that the sense of community among convicts is very strong.

On another occasion, in his closed cell, he heard the screams of an inmate being beaten by guards. Unable to endure the man's sufferings, he began to drum on his cell door with both fists. Other prisoners took up the protest, pounding on a dozen doors along the corridor. Mindszenty's cell was opened by the guards. He expected them to continue where they had left off, using him as their whipping boy. But at least on this occasion they did not touch him. If they had, he felt certain that the enraged prisoners would have resumed their drumming in sympathy and protest.

Despite what he suffered at the hands of those who guarded him, the cardinal had the fairness to record in his memoirs that these officers were cogs in a great machine and oftentimes as much imprisoned by the system as those who were behind bars. He lists several incidents in which they shared moments of God's grace:

> In 1949, at the very time that hatred was dominant, an auxiliary policeman slipped into my cell when the others were already asleep, looked around cautiously and whispered: "Father, trust in God! He helps!"
>
> Later he came to comfort me a second time. The third time he came to bid goodbye for he was being transferred.
>
> . . . In 1954, toward the end of my stay in the penitentiary, the stocky little sergeant whose duty it was to take me to the bath, looked at me one day, peered at the door, then murmured: "I am a Christian, too."
>
> . . . A barber in the prison hospital proudly told me that his daughter was receiving religious instruction and that he had gone to midnight Mass with her.[2]

Mindszenty remained in prison until 1956, when the Hungarian populace arose in revolt against their communist overlords.

---

2. Mindszenty, *Memoirs*, 177.

Mindszenty was freed, but after a brief respite of liberty, he was forced to take refuge in the US embassy as Soviet troops massed into the country and crushed the revolt. He lived within the confines of the legation for the next fifteen years. In 1971 he was taken from Hungary to Vienna where, in 1975, he died in exile from his homeland.

For those who lived through the Cold War at its coldest, Cardinal Mindszenty's name became a symbol of communist oppression of religion and human liberty. It is for a different reason, however, that he is included in these sketches. While in prison he experienced and expressed a oneness with all who were incarcerated, regardless of why they were behind bars. He also learned to appreciate that they were ordinary folk, and that, despite his position as a member of the College of Cardinals within the church's hierarchy, he too was ordinary folk with them. He decided that no matter how it is that "the political left" has been given to hero worship of prisoners, the truth is that someone who has done time in prison becomes neither a villain nor a hero. He had experienced that the great daily struggle for all who are imprisoned is the fight to maintain some semblance of human dignity. He had joined them in that struggle.

In his years in prison Mindszenty observed as well that the natural community which prisoners shared was deepened when there was shared faith. He noted:

> Prison was certainly no bulwark against sin; only grace and good will are that. Nevertheless I do believe that in prison the heavenly Father confers his grace more generously. He knows best all the things we need in our situation. In the cell, as everywhere, the spiritual life grew and flourished only if the prisoner himself tended it. But if there were several men together, and perhaps a priest among them, the religious life did attain a high point in prison.[3]

The cardinal, in the context of communist persecutions, is referring to the presence of priests among inmates as fellow inmates.

3. Mindszenty, *Memoirs*, 180.

Nonetheless it is a reminder of the importance of the ministry of faith communities to the incarcerated. There are many jails situated in the shadow of churches in our country that never experience the presence of clergy. Oftentimes clergy, living within the vicinity of jails, balm their own conscience by saying that they are "on call" if an inmate ever asks to see them.

Many inmates, already experiencing a sense of alienation from the community that jailed them, will not dare to ask even when they are most in need. It is the personal sharing of God's grace within their midst that makes the difference. This on the authority of inmate Jozsef Mindszenty.

Chapter 4

Sparrows on Housetops
Dorothy Day—Saint Therese of Lisieux

IN THE LATE 1890S a Carmelite nun dying of tuberculosis while still in her early twenties was asked by her superior to record in a journal her reflections upon her own life and her spirituality, which she called the "little way." It was a reality based upon heroic virtue in the smallest situations of everyday life. Typical of this heroism was a passage wherein, while sitting in a wheelchair in the convent's garden, the invalid endured continual interruptions by well-meaning sisters as she attempted to accomplish the task given to her:

> I can't put down my thoughts properly unless I'm as lonely as a sparrow on the housetop, and this isn't a common experience. The moment I take up my pen to write, one of the dear sisters comes along with a pitchfork on her shoulder, passing close by me—a little chat, she thinks, would do me good . . . At last I get tired of opening and shutting the famous autobiography, and open a book instead.[1]

The first editions of the posthumous work were issued without any identification of the author. The public sought her identity and the sisters finally revealed it. Born Therese Martin, she had

1. Therese of Lisieux, *Autobiography of a Soul*, 274.

been given by the Carmelites at Lisieux the religious name Therese of the Child Jesus. Devotion to her as "the Little Flower" immediately bloomed throughout the church. Rome was moved to waive the customary period of fifty years before considering sanctity; in 1925 she was declared a saint. Pope Pius XI called her impact on the world "a hurricane of Glory."[2]

New York activist Dorothy Day, wrestling with her own ambivalent feelings about the Catholic Church as she was entering it, followed a suggestion that she look at the autobiography of Therese of the Child Jesus.

Day experienced jail cells from the inside each time she was arrested for espousing radical causes—and had an ever-lengthening rap sheet kept in police and court files. In her autobiography *The Long Loneliness* she would write:

> I do not know how sincere I was in my love of the poor and my desire to serve them . . . I wanted to go on picket lines, to go to jail, to write, to influence others and so make my mark on the world.[3]

She was at the same age as Saint Therese of the Child Jesus was when she resolved to continue to do the work she had done on earth while in heaven. Dorothy couldn't wait that long; she would do her work on earth, sheltering the homeless and leading radical causes into her eighties. A wonderful set of newspaper photos from the early 1980s shows her in her last year of life as she joined in protesting on behalf of farm workers attempting to unionize. Arrested and jailed yet again, she is surrounded by young police officers, guns in their belts, while she, owing to frailty of age, is sitting on a provided plastic chair. A young woman officer standing next to her looks like she wants to say, "Dear God, I'm arresting my grandmother."

Again, at the same age as when "The Little Flower" wrote her spiritual memoirs, Dorothy was arrested while rallying with suffragettes in Washington, DC, and was sentenced to thirty days in

2. Rohrbach, "St. Therese of Lisieux," 78.

3. Day, *Long Loneliness*, 70.

jail—her first incarceration. While she was there she recorded her own spiritual memoirs as she experienced a reality that lay beyond her middle-class, sheltered imagination. For an activist such as herself, just sitting still in a cell was torture enough.

"The first six days of inactivity were as six thousand years," she wrote, "Another torture was the lack of privacy: there was a toilet in each cell, open, and paper and flushing was supplied by the guard. It was as though one were in a zoo with the open bars leading into the corridor."

Jail was a normal way of life for street people incarcerated repeatedly for small offenses:

"These prisoners kept up their chatter after 8 o'clock, and the matron kept puffing around the place trying to quell the giggling, singing and quarreling. The men and women were separated, but I saw sex and felt it at its crudest."[4]

It is likely that the sheltered Therese Martin never laid eyes on a jail building. Yet a murderer convicted of killing in circumstances that the press and society at large deemed unforgivable did much to bring Therese to the realization of her great mission in life and in eternity.

In 1887, a woman, her maid, and a twelve-year-old girl were found murdered in a house on the Rue Montaigne in Paris. Shortly afterwards, a tall, handsome man was arrested in Marseilles attempting to sell jewelry that had belonged to one of the victims. An Egyptian-born Italian, Henri Pranzini was a drifter whose one great talent was a facility for a number of languages. Though he stoutly maintained his innocence, the trial was sensationalized in newspapers and public opinion was raged against him. He was condemned to the guillotine.

The atmosphere in the Martin home was protective to the extent that Therese's widowed father, a jeweler and watchmaker, discouraged his daughters from reading newspapers. The Pranzini case, however, was the heated topic of the day, and the Martin girls heard it discussed continually.

4. Day, *The Long Loneliness*, 77–78.

Fourteen-year-old Therese was drawn toward Pranzini not because she thought him a sympathetic figure but precisely because he was despicable and despised. He was a soul, and his salvation was at stake. She began to pray for him and to offer for his behalf personal sacrifices. His reclamation became a singular mission for her. She wanted to have a Mass said for him, and, needing assistance in this, confided in her older sister Celine, who became her co-missionary for the sake of Pranzini. Awaiting execution, he was steadfast in refusing the ministrations of the prison chaplain.

Therese increased her concentration in prayer. Later, she wrote:

> I was convinced in the depths of my heart that our desires would be granted, but to give me courage to go on praying for sinners I told God I was sure he would pardon poor unfortunate Pranzini and that I would believe it even if he did not go to confession or show any sign of repentance. I had such confidence in Jesus' infinite mercy, but I was asking for a "sign" of repentance, just for my own consolation.[5]

The day after the execution, she risked her father's disapproval by reading *La Croix*, combing through the newspaper accounts for the sign she sought. She found it. Pranzini had continued to ignore the chaplain who accompanied him to the guillotine. Then suddenly, at the last moment as he was being strapped to the board under the great knife, he suddenly gestured to the priest, took the crucifix from him, and kissed the wounds on the figure of Christ.

Therese felt a sense of security first for Pranzini. "Here was this man," she wrote, "the first child of my prayers, as you might call him, dying with those sacred wounds pressed closely to his lips."[6]

She felt just as secure that this gesture had been the sign from heaven which she had begged for. It affirmed her in her sense of mission. "After that special grace," she resolved, "my longing to save souls grew from day to day."[7]

5. Therese of Lisieux, *Autobiography of a Soul*, 105–6.

6. Therese of Lisieux, *Autobiography of a Soul*, 106.

7. Therese of Lisieux, *Autobiography of a Soul*, 33.

She spent her life in the convent praying for others. Nor did she ever forget that Pranzini was her "first child." Whenever she had the opportunity to have a Mass intention she requested that it be for him. Before she died, Therese resolved that her intercession for others would not end with her death. With the happy presumption of the truly innocent, she did not worry about whether she was going to be received into heaven, but rather planned on what she would do there.

"I want to spend my heaven doing good on earth," she declared.[8]

Perhaps many of us should admit that we venerate Saint Therese, the "Little Flower," not so much out of admiration for her purity of heart, but out of our own self-serving. Since she announced that she was going to spend heaven doing good on earth, those of us with a vending-machine view of praying see her as an easy touch for intercession. But we should be forewarned. Her power of prayer was part of the whole package of her attitude towards others, even murderers. We want favors from heaven without having these same attitudes. Oftentimes ignoring the fact that we tell God to forgive us our trespasses as we forgive those who trespass against us we forget as well that immediately after the "Our Father" in Matthew's Gospel, Jesus underlines this with a warning: "If you forgive others the wrongs they have done you, your Father in heaven will also forgive you. But if you do not forgive others, the Father will not forgive the wrongs you have done" (Matt 8:14–15).

Years after she wrote the above rejection of Saint Therese's love of the incarcerated, Dorothy Day wrote: "It took me a longer time to realize the unique position of Therese of Lisieux in the Church today."[9]

That she did realize it eventually is consistent with the growth of her own life in the Spirit and in prayer. She decided that "in these days of fear and trembling of what man has wrought on earth

8. Therese of Lisieux, *Autobiography of a Soul*, 105.

9. Day, *Therese*, vii.

in destructiveness and hate, Therese is the saint we need."[10] She penned her own biography of the saint's life, explaining:

> I write to overcome the sense of futility in Catholics, men, women and youths, married and single, who feel hopeless and useless, less than the dust, ineffectual, wasted, powerless. On the one hand Theresa was "the little grain of sand" and the other "her name was written in heaven." She was a little less than the angels, and so are we all.[11]

10. Day, *Therese*, vii.
11. Day, *Therese*, viii.

Chapter 5

Willing to Save the Condemned

THERE WERE MANY SIMILARITIES between the nineteenth century of Therese and the fourteenth century for Catherine of Siena. Both had a direct and simple relationship with God, both died while still young, both were born into large families (Therese was the youngest of nine children, Catherine the twenty-third of twenty-five), and both were raised in a gentle and sheltered atmosphere. When Catherine's sister, Bonaventura, newly married, was exposed for the first time in her life to the crudity of masculine swearing, she angrily confronted her young husband and his companions and told them: "In my father's house I was never used to hearing such talk, and if you do not want to see me dead soon, I beg of you to cease this filthy chatter."[1]

Catherine took vows as a Third Order Dominican while still a teenager, continuing to live in her parents' home. As young as she was her reputation grew as a mystic. Men and women seeking spiritual direction gathered about her and, though oftentimes older than her in years, affectionately called her "Momma."

Her teachings were eventually gathered into a volume, the *Dialogues*, which stands today as one of the great treasures of

1. Jørgensen, *Saint Catherine of Siena*, 2.

Western mysticism. Yet Catherine did not live in an age which seemed a likely setting for the luxury of mysticism. The historian Barbara Tuchman in *A Distant Mirror* labeled the era "the calamitous fourteenth century," an age of political and natural disasters capped by the Black Death and the splitting of the church into factions led by rival popes.

So Little of the Virtue of Meekness

Catherine did not shrink from involvement in this world. She lost members of her family to the plague and became dangerously ill herself while nursing others. More significantly, she involved herself in politics, earning enemies with her strength of will and strength of expressing it. In 1374 charges by such enemies forced her to defend her orthodoxy before a General Chapter of the Dominican Order.

"God wills and I will . . ." was her unblinking way of beginning a disputation. This assertiveness would later rankle her biographers as much as it did her contemporaries. One of them, Michael de la Bedoyere, observed: "No other great saint, to my knowledge, has shown so little of the virtue of meekness, even of humility, as the terms are understood."[2]

One person who felt the sting of her lack of meekness was Pope Gregory XI, and because he felt it, so too did the entire papal court. That court was in comfortable French Avignon rather than in Rome, rundown, squalid Rome, at this point in time. Catherine first wrote to the pope of her displeasure about this, and then betook herself to Avignon to complain in person. At first, small of stature and dressed in the simplicity of her religious habit (this considered an eccentricity by the papal retinue), she was the butt of smiles and jokes. The laughter stopped when the pope started to pack, beaten down by her arguments that he had to return to the See of Saint Peter.

2. de la Bedoyere, *Catherine, Saint of Siena*, 231.

It is notable that de la Bedoyere, who had groused about Catherine's lack of meekness, saw a balance to this lack. He wrote: "Rare are the souls who can take life as seriously as Catherine did, but rarer still are those who can do this and not lose the common touch of our pathetic and petty lives and social relations."[3]

My Dear Sons in Christ

Catherine would be declared a saint by the Catholic Church not because of her political prowess but because the ordinary people of Siena who loved her wanted to call her saint. She was constant not only in her care of the sick and the poor but of prisoners; not only of political prisoners who were unjustly incarcerated, but of criminals justly convicted. She would remain with those condemned to death throughout the entire night before their execution, preparing them to meet both death and eternity with hope. In a letter to inmates written to encourage them to receive Holy Communion, and written before she was thirty years of age herself, she addresses them as "My dearest sons in Christ sweet Jesus."

She draws for them a parallel between their own sufferings and the insults and tortures endured by Christ. Describing the Lord in chivalry imagery as a knight whose wounds were his armor, she encourages Christ's fellow convicts, saying: "We must follow Him that in Him we may find consolation in all our trials and afflictions."[4]

I Received His Head into My Hands

Her greatest test with the incarcerated came with the case of Niccolo di Toldo, condemned to be beheaded for having spoken out at a banquet against the city fathers of Siena. Totally unchurched, never even having received his first communion, he refused to let any priest into his cell. Strong-willed Catherine entered instead

3. de la Bedoyere, *Catherine, Saint of Siena*, 220.

4. Jørgensen, *Saint Catherine of Siena*, 257.

and adopted him as her own. She brought him to the Christian sacraments for the first time in his life. A child to her, he finally leaned his head against her breast the night before he was to die, and expressed his fear that he might not be able to accept death without her.

"Stay with me and don't leave me," he pleaded, "then I shall be alright and die happy."

She promised him that she would be with him the next day. In the morning she went alone to the place of execution. It was something that society forbade women to do, but Catherine lived a life beyond the expectations of society. In order to feel what Niccolo would experience she went to the block, knelt, and placed her own neck upon it. She prayed, praying to (and with) another woman for Niccolo in terms consistent with her personality:

"I begged, indeed forced Mary to get me the grace I wanted, which was that I might give him light and peace of heart at the moment of death, and then see him going to God. I was so absorbed in the assurance I received that my prayer would be granted that I saw no one in the crowd around me."

When the executioners arrived with Niccolo, he saw her and smiled. She made the sign of the cross over him, and prayed with him. She herself bared his neck after he knelt and held his head in her hands while he kept whispering: "Jesus . . . Catherine." The blade fell and his life's blood splattered onto her. Seeing beyond the physical horror of the moment, she experienced what she felt the Virgin Mary had promised her; she experienced Niccolo's soul being received into heaven. Characteristic of Catherine's blending of heaven's grace with her own strong personality, she recorded this mystic and earthly experience by saying: "I received his head into my hands while my eyes were fixed on the divine goodness as I said, 'I will.'"[5]

∾

5. Catherine of Siena, *I, Catherine*, 71.

My own home state, New York, has not inflicted the death penalty since 1963. Yet, it is something I need to deal with when inmates sentenced to death in other states are housed here because of other charges in this jurisdiction. One such man convicted of robbery/murder in another state and sentenced to death was brought back to face a robbery/murder charge in his home state.

He spent many months in a jail where I serve.

In crime and in personality he would be closer to Maria Goretti's murderer rather than to the embittered young political prisoner befriended by Catherine of Siena. There was no way of minimizing his robbery murders, nor is there any way of prettifying a life spent in drug dealing and ongoing career crime.

Every experience in life, from childhood on, had conspired to solidify and freeze his attitude in this respect. He could not fit the idea of a loving God into any reality he had known since birth. Not stupid by any means, he would read well and enjoy talking at length about almost anything under the sun—other than religion. Religion, especially organized religion, remained a major turnoff for him. Almost out of a dutiful politeness he agreed to take a copy of the New Testament from me and then allow himself to get into discussions about it.

On my part I found myself beset by an inexplicable exhaustion after every conversation with him. Never for a moment whenever I spoke with him did his appointment with death escape my mind or my emotions. It made me feel responsible for steering him both by prayer and talk toward a connection with God, and I was continually depressed that I could not seem to move him anywhere in that direction. He never minimized his crime or situation ("I know what I did. I'm not asking for anything special.") and he stoutly insisted that there was no good in addressing the situation to any notion of the existence of a good God who might possibly care about people.

His only evident emotional soft spot was for his early-school-age son. Once, on a special visit, when his family members were the only people in the jail's visiting area, I accidentally dropped my plastic swipe card which is run through the computer clock whenever I enter and exit the facility. It doesn't open any gates and it would never get anyone out of the building, but when the boy swooped down, picked up the card, and handed it to me his father grimaced, slapped a hand to his forehead and groaned, "Now, why did you go and do that? We could have got me out of this place with that."

Even the small boy, like his father no dummy, knew better and laughed with the rest of us. The small moment of levity allowed for the only trace of real merriment which we had shared.

A couple of weeks after that the boy was beaten up in a schoolyard by older boys mocking his father. When his father heard what had happened to him he was visibly shaken, the only time I had seen him so. The child was subsequently taken out of the public school where he had been and enrolled in a parish school where it was hoped that he would be more protected by the environment.

"It's more than him just being safe," his father admitted. He added hesitantly, "I . . . I want him to know about God."

Shortly after this he was shipped back to the state where he was sentenced. As of this writing he still sits on death row there and likely will stay on death row until he dies of old age. I witnessed no great conversion of the sort that might interest a dramatist in his story. But I also have no doubt that God is in quiet dialogue with him in his soul and that he is opening himself to listen.

Chapter 6

Saint Francis, the Street Brawler

THE FACTS AND MYTHS about the life of Francis of Assisi are fairly well known. The great majority of stories told about him emphasize his life after his conversion. It is rarely mentioned that in his youth he was held for a year in what Thomas of Celano, his contemporary and first biographer, described as "the squalor of a prison." He was not imprisoned for defending his faith but for taking part in what that same author labeled as "a bloody battle between the citizens of Perugia and those of Assisi."[1]

These small, neighboring cities were set on hills within sight of each other; thus the issue between them was not a matter of war between differing national groups. This was the age of feudalism. Principal cities of the Italian peninsula had been held by German overlords. In an eruption of independence and class warfare, the citizens of Assisi had torn down the castle stronghold of their overlord, Conrad of Swabia. Using the bricks of his castle, they built a protective wall around their city and turned against the remaining nobility in the vicinity. Those nobles who did not accept the new order of things fled to neighboring Perugia, whose nobility gave

---

1. Thomas of Celano, "First Life of Saint Francis," 71–75.

them sanctuary. This was the cause of the hostilities that broke out between the two communities in 1202.

Given the presence of Germanic invaders in Italy, the fight between fellow Italians seems senseless, but as historian Paul Sabatier observed in his biography of Francis: "The rivalries of the cities were too strong for them to see that local liberty without a common independence is precarious and illusory."[2]

Francis Beradone was then nineteen or twenty years of age. Thomas of Celano's assessment of the saint's pre-conversion personality is as close as we can get in time to an accurate portrait. He informs us that the adolescent Francis was "flighty and not a little rash." He strove among his admiring companions "to outdo the rest in the pomp of vainglory, in jokes, in strange doings, in idle and useless talk, in songs, in soft and flowing garments, for he was very rich; not however avaricious but prodigal, not a hoarder of money but a squander-er of his possessions . . . On the other hand, he was a very kindly person, easy and affable, even making himself foolish because of it."[3]

Having been raised on the legends of King Arthur and his Knights of the Round Table, he longed not so much for battle itself, but for the resulting "pomp and vainglory." He joined a group of youths from Assisi in a fight with a band of Perugians at the bridge of San Giovanni, spanning a stream which separated the two cities. In scope, this melee between neighbors was not so much like a battle reminiscent of *Camelot* as a gang brawl out of *West Side Story*. When it was done with, Francis, along with the other young men from Assisi, were arrested by the authorities of Perugia and held in prison for a year.

In no way can this imprisonment be counted as one of the reasons why he would someday be canonized as a saint. The young man simply "did time" for being in a bloody street brawl, now behind bars, experiencing a total loss of personal liberty. Living within this closed society that is a world unto itself, Francis played the role taken by at least one inmate on every tier, that of the clown

2. Sabatier, *Life of Saint Francis*, 364.
3. Thomas of Celano, "First Life of Saint Francis," 230.

looking for laughs. Once everyone gets down to simply living life inside a prison a certain gallows humor surfaces. People need to laugh. Some inmates seem inordinate in their enjoyment of the prison life.

Francis Beradone chose to play this same clown role while he was behind bars. Thomas of Celano tell us that this was the role he had played throughout his adolescence: "in jokes, in strange doings . . . making himself foolish because of it." He tells us as well that in prison some of his fellow inmates "resented his happiness and considered him insane and mad."[4]

Francis spun out a defense of his merriment for the sake of his critics.

"I rejoice," he told his fellow inmates, "because someday I shall be venerated as a saint all over the world."[5]

History measures these words in light of his later life and labels them prophetic. Had Francis remained as much a fool as he was thought to be at that moment, his boast would only stand witness that he was unduly enamored with himself. Neither Francis himself nor any of the first Franciscan biographers ever attempted to place any value in his prison experience. He simply did time.

Yet, if he thought too much of himself, he was, even then, naturally openhearted toward others as well. Once in his father's shop he had waved away a beggar who bothered him while he was busy. Suddenly, catching himself in his cold hardheartedness, he ran out into the street after the beggar and begged his forgiveness. In prison, one man locked in with Francis was a knight who had a particularly negative personality. In reaction the others shunned him. Francis, just as he had run after the beggar, befriended the man and gradually made him a part of the community.

But again, his befriending of the knight, much like his self-canonizing prophecy, can be given a less than saintly spin. Prisons are often referred to as "gladiator schools." Society takes youngsters who have committed minor initial offenses and puts them in cell blocks with professionals who can really teach them the trade.

4. Thomas of Celano, "Second Life of Saint Francis," 364.

5. Green, *God's Fool*, 48.

Veteran of a puny brawl at a bridge, Francis wanted the glory of real battles in real wars. He would later say that he once had a dream wherein he saw himself surrounded by armor and weaponry that belonged to him and to his followers. When he befriended the knight in prison his motives may have been to ingratiate himself with a master of the trade. They would not always remain behind bars; and here was a professional warrior who could show Francis the way to war.

After a year's time, when the prisoners were released, Francis did put on expensive armor to join the Papal army, which, under the command of Walter of Brienne, was campaigning to free the Italian peninsula of German forces. The expensive armor did not last long. With his typical wholeheartedness, Francis gave it away to yet another impoverished knight. Then, while still en route to join the main forces of the army, he experienced a troubling dream in which he heard a voice ask him:

"Tell me, Francis, who can benefit you most: the lord or the servant?"

When he answered, "The lord," the voice, in turn, responded:

"Then why do you desert the lord for the servant?"[6]

The gradual process of his conversion had begun.

Francis did enter into a true penitentiary experience after his release. Led by the grace of Christ who embraced lepers, he forced himself to embrace a leper because lepers were particularly loathsome to him. He then volunteered to work regularly in a hospital for those stricken by the disease.

This God-voiced task was given to a young man who had a rap sheet that included gang warfare and a year in prison, even his father disowning him. Francis returned to his father all his rich clothing and for the rest of his life wore only the rough, brown, sack-like wool clothing of a beggar.

For posterity's sake, Francis of Assisi, in later life, recalled each slow step he took in his process of turning to Christ; the above-mentioned dream, a serious illness that took hold of him, his personal, loving acceptance of lepers, and, above all, his great

6. Delaney, *Dictionary*, 234.

mystical experience in front of a crucifix in the abandoned chapel of San Damiano, the Lord ordering, "Francis, rebuild my church, which as you see is in ruins."[7]

The church was in a dead end of its own making—under the reign of the most powerful, secular pope in history, war-bent Innocent III, who massacred groups such as the Cathars that he decided were heretical and who called for a fifth crusade to continue centuries of constant warfare in an attempt to reconquer the "Holy Land" from Islamic forces that held it in possession. One would have thought the church was in full glory given such human power. Instead, Jesus tells Francis that "it is in ruins."

In his adolescence Francis had wanted to wear armor and go to war. This time he wanted to go to the world war called the Crusades not to gain glory for himself but to bring peace. With several other friars, he went to Egypt, where many nations of the world were fighting for possession and control. Francis walked through the battle lines, amazingly not getting killed, and was taken into custody by the ruler of Egypt, Sultan Malik al Kamil.

The two men were the same age. They were both men of deep faith, and they were both poets with a love for God. It was an immediate friendship, Francis hoping he would bring Malik to belief in Christ. After several more days of talking about peace and how to bring it about, Sultan Malik got a momentary truce so that Francis could return across to the other side of the battlefield.

Sultan Malik al Kamil habitually asked spiritual leaders and poets to write down copies of their works. This collection included prayers and poetry and has made their writings a treasure trove to this present day. One wonders if any of it might include writings Francis may have given to him in their discussions about faith. Early collections of these would include "Canticle of the Sun," "Praises of the Creatures," "Joyfully Praising God," and "Brother Sun; Sister Moon."

Any collection of Francis's poetry and prayers include a beautiful moment when a large flock of birds filled tree branches,

---

7. Thomas of Celano, "Second Life of Francis," 335.

trusting in the gentleness of the scene as Francis spoke to a crowd of people. Francis rejoiced at their presence:

"Birds of the sky, you are bound to heaven, to God your creator. In every beat of your wings and every note of your songs praise him. He has given you the greatest gift, freedom of the air. You neither sow nor reap, yet God provides for you the most delicious food, rivers and lakes to quench your thirst, mountains and valleys for your home . . . clearly our creator loves you dearly—and gives you the most beautiful clothing; a change of feathers every season."[8]

It is a reflection of Jesus in the Gospels using the example of birds and asking, "Are not two sparrows sold for a penny? Yet not one of them will fall to the ground apart from your father . . . Do not be afraid; you are of more value than many sparrows . . . It is not the will of your heavenly Father that one of them be lost" (Matt 10:29–31; 18:14).

One thinks of the criminal Dismas, dying on the cross next to the cross of Christ, and jailbird Francis, momentarily a fallen sparrow reclaimed by God.

The most well-known prayer attributed to Francis is the prayer, "Make me an instrument of your peace." Yet there is no record of Francis ever praying or using it.

The prayer first surfaces in the early twentieth century. In 1912, in Paris, it was printed in a devotional/thought-for-the-day pamphlet put together by a parish priest—Fr. Esther Bouquerel. He might well have been the prayer's author.

The prayer, phrased much as we know it, was passed about during World War I.

Many seminarians of my age group were told—usually by our peer seminarians from New York City—that the "Peace Prayer" was written by tough-knuckled "Francis" Cardinal Spellman of that city during World War II when he was military vicar of the armed forces. Throughout the war he had millions of copies of the prayer printed and distributed as a prayer for peace. Little wonder that some think he was the prayer's author.

---

8. Francis of Assisi, *Little Flowers*.

A more likely candidate is Brother Giles—one of the first members of the Franciscan Order. He was a local farmer in Assisi who left his fields to follow Francis. Francis always called him "Knight of Our Round Table." Giles wrote a prayer that is a near likeness of the Instrument of Peace prayer:

Blessed is he who loves and does not therefore desire to be loved,
Blessed is he who fears and does not therefore desire to be feared,
Blessed is he who serves and therefore does not desire to be served,
Blessed is he who behaves well toward others,
and does not desire that others behave well to him,
And because these are great things the foolish do not rise to them.

The Peace Prayer of Saint Francis
Lord, make me an instrument of your peace:
where there is hatred, let me sow love;
where there is injury, pardon;
where there is doubt, faith;
where there is despair, hope;
where there is darkness, light:
where there is sadness, joy.
O divine Master,
grant that I may so much seek
to be consoled as to console;
to be understood as to understand,
to be loved as to love.
For it is in giving that we receive;
it is in pardoning that we are pardoned,
it is in dying that we are born to eternal life.[9]

Whether or not Francis wrote it, it gives a profound portrait of a saint who began his career as a fallen sparrow.

9. Klein, "Peace Prayer."

Chapter 7

The Gallows Priest and His Hanged Saints

THE SHOCKING THEOLOGICAL STATEMENT, "God would pardon even the devils if they repented and asked forgiveness," was made not by a present-day extreme liberal, but by an austere, self-disciplined mid-nineteenth-century priest who was a moral theologian and then rector at an ecclesiastical college in Turin, Italy.

Joseph Cafasso has been canonized as a saint by the church, along with his student, protege, and first biographer John (Don) Bosco.[1] Unlike Don Bosco, who remained boyishly attractive even into old age, Cafasso's already puny frame was further dwarfed by a twisted spine and hunched right shoulder, the results of a crippling childhood bout with rickets. Nevertheless, giving evidence that physical attributes weigh little in long-range evaluations by others, Cafasso was, throughout his life, not merely popular but beloved by the general populace of Turin. His great fame was as a gentle confessor, and in this capacity it was his habit to spend almost every morning hearing confessions, oftentimes doing so from 6 a.m. to noon.

---

1. Jalbert, *Walk While You Have the Light*, 31.

He advised the young priests under his tutelage to be sure to enter the confessional with a happy countenance, lest a severe expression scare away hesitant penitents. When other priests claimed that people came to him because he gave easy penances, he answered: "If they get hard penances they might not come back to confession at all. What a loss that will be for them."

Even young Don Bosco with his sunlit personality thought that Cafasso was too soft and reminded his teacher that the Bible taught "narrow is the door."

"What of it?" Cafasso shrugged. "Just so we get in. It isn't necessary that we go two abreast. The Scriptures don't say that we can't enter but that some don't enter."[2]

Lenient with others, he was rigid with himself. "The body is insatiable," he would say, "The more we give it the more it demands." Don Bosco, who knew him for thirty-two years, said that he never saw him play cards, billiards, checkers or chess. He avoided displays of affection, and, as Bosco observed, "He never smelled flowers." It almost sounds like the present-day observation that some people never take time to smell the roses. Perhaps Cafasso was too hard on his own body and psyche. Giving always to others and allowing nothing to himself, he burnt out his energies and died, exhausted, at the age of forty-nine.[3]

Stopping to Smell the Jail Tiers

From the first days of his priesthood until his death he served as chaplain at Turin's four penal institutions and was present at so many public executions he was called "the gallows priest." The great theme of his ministry, one which reflected his gentleness with all penitents, was that he was not to "save" criminals as if they were a lesser order of humans. He insisted upon making heroes of his repentant inmates, and when they were executed hailed them as "hanged holy ones," saints of the church triumphant in heaven.

2. Hutchinson, *Diocesan Priest Saints*, 33.

3. Hutchinson, *Diocesan Priest Saints*, 38.

It was no less repulsive to some of his contemporaries than would be a similar claim by a present-day death row chaplain who would insist that repentant, executed murders are saints.[4]

Like many prison chaplains, Cafasso had to earn his credibility both with inmates and with the authorities. His life spanned the age of Italy's unification, during which time the church, holding onto political authority in the Papal States, was seen as a major obstacle to political progress. It was an era of sometimes violent anti-clericalism. During one revolutionary upheaval Pope Pius IX had to flee from Rome disguised as a monk. In Turin the archbishop was exiled, and when government authorities suspected that Cafasso, as rector of St. Francis Theological College, possessed a forbidden letter from him, the whole college, and Cafasso's room in particular, were carefully searched. But this was late in the chaplain's career, and he had learned a lot of street smarts from his clientele. After the police left empty-handed, he smiled to his students and said:

"They can't catch the priest of the gallows like that."[5]

His small size and hunched posture were an added disability in a ministry where teenage inmates greeted the arrival of any priest with derision and crow-like cries of "caw, caw." He was still new to the job when he responded to the request of one inmate who asked him to come to see him on his tier. As the priest entered the area, the young man, from above him, dumped a bucket of filthy water on him. Cafasso proceeded to visit with him as if nothing had happened.

The older, hardened inmates saw little in him that might inspire confidence. A murderer who towered over him greeted his presence by saying:

"What do you want in here, little man? I have already turned down a number of priests, all better than yourself. Don't you know that with two little fingers around your neck I could strangle you?"

Cafasso stood his ground and began his response by saying:

"I'm not afraid of you."

Taken aback, the inmate finally announced:

4. Phelan, *Don Bosco*, 61.
5. Jalbert, *Walk While You Have the Light*, 20.

"I suppose I have to give in to this little priest and do what he wants."

What he wanted was to bring him to God; and he did. The man became so attached to "this little priest" that he insisted that Cafasso sit with him in his cell on the day of his execution, as well as accompany him to the gallows.[6]

Confessional Style

In time Cafasso won most of them over. He made it a point to make friends of guards who soon felt it unnecessary to bar him from entering any of the areas of the prisons and with executioners who soon made sure that he knew when hangings were scheduled so that he could be present for the sake of the condemned. In his own way he out-toughed the toughest of the prisoners. On a particular feast day the inhabitants of one cell block had promised to him that they would go to confession. When he arrived on the tier they had changed their minds and hung back. He walked over to them, stood in front of one man, then reached up with both hands and grabbed his beard. This initiated the following dialogue:

"Let go of my beard."

"I won't let go until you go to confession."

"But . . . I don't want to go to confession."

"Say what you want. I'll not let you go until you give in."

"I'm not ready."

"I'll prepare you."

The man went to confession and then convinced the others to follow his example.[7]

Another example of his confessional style occurred when an inmate, kneeling to confess, suddenly felt ashamed of what he had to tell. He started to rise. Cafasso grabbed him. They grappled.

6. Hutchinson, *Diocesan Priest Saints*, 37.

7. Jalbert, *Walk While You Have the Light*, 195.

Both men fell and rolled about on the floor. The man finished confessing. What were his other options?[8]

Basically Shy

It is fascinating to compare the austerity and unsocial lifestyle of Cafasso outside the prisons to his adaption to a rough and tumble world within them. He would agree that he felt totally comfortable with prisoners even though he was not comfortable in ordinary society.

Even his physical actions when behind bars became fluid and quick. Once, he discovered that he had been pickpocketed of his tobacco and announced in mock horror to the inmates around him:

"Is it possible that there are robbers here?"[9]

Cafasso was traveling with his brother outside Turin once when they were held up on the road by a robber. As the man demanded their cash, he suddenly recognized his chaplain from prison and apologized profusely. The priest insisted upon giving him some money to tide him over. Many years later this reformed robber was to testify of this incident to church officials investigating Cafasso's cause for canonization.[10]

One of Cafasso's constant worries in his prison ministry was that he might be caught in a situation where, because of the secrets he knew, he'd be thought to be an informer. Knowing of plans of one proposed escape, he panicked when no escape attempt was made. He wondered if the men had held off because they thought he had said something. As it turned out, an inmate was discovered to be an informer. But it shows the delicateness of the position in which a chaplain is placed.

Sometimes the compromising situation in which Cafasso was placed was of his own making. Pietro Mottino, who led a Robin Hood existence at the head of a band of robbers, counted Cafasso

8. Jalbert, *Walk While You Have the Light*, 195.

9. Jalbert, *Walk While You Have the Light*, 142.

10. Jalbert, *Walk While You Have the Light*, 142.

as a friend and showed up at his dwelling twice, though an arrest meant a sentence of death. The feeling of affection was obviously mutual, for on these occasions Cafasso not only met with him; he served him dinner, and did so in a garden area near a wall so that Mottino could make a quick escape should the police arrive at the door. Pietro was eventually captured, and, at the age of twenty-seven, ended his career on the gallows. No doubt deeply grieving for this man for whom he felt personal affection, Cafasso was at his side as the noose was put around his neck.[11]

The chaplain leaned heavily upon the help of others in his ministry behind the prison walls, including help given him by the prisoners. Giovanni da Cambiano was a long-term inmate who had been won over by the priest. He became as valued an assistant as would have been a loyal cleric or sacristan at the theological college. Nicknamed by the other prisoners "Ravveduto"—"the penitent"—he kept his eye out for those who were in special need of the chaplain's ministrations and steered Cafasso to them. Like the robber who was given money by Cafasso, Cambiano, many years later, gave testimony before the Vatican commission studying the priest's case for canonization.[12]

Disciples in Chaplaincy

Cafasso also used the student priests in his charge for help, bringing them into the prisons with him as part of their training. The instructions he gave them reflected his own long experience and his compassionate understanding for the weaknesses of human nature. The inmates, he told them, were to be treated as "gentlemen."

"Never be offended if they deceive you," he said, "and never denounce them for [their crimes], as their lot is already hard enough. Never ask them why they are in prison, for naturally they are all perfectly innocent."[13]

---

11. Jørgensen, *Don Bosco*, 80.

12. Jalbert, *Walk While You Have the Light*, 121.

13. Jørgensen, *Don Bosco*, 57.

In a statement strange only if one has never worked with individuals ready to claim that society has martyred them, he advised the student priests:

"Don't speak about the passion of Our Lord, his capture, his bonds, for the men are apt to compare themselves to the savior and say that they, too, are being treated unjustly."[14]

Now, at the Hour of Our Death

As an acid test of their preparation in this ministry he would even have the young priests accompany doomed men to their execution. One such student priest could not stomach the scene, became ill, and nearly fainted. Cafasso, who was accompanying another inmate to execution, replaced him and took care of both prisoners. The young priest was John Bosco. This student, who was to share canonization with his teacher even though he could not share the same hard duties, recorded for posterity his mentor's method of preparing the condemned for death. He wrote:

> No sooner had Don Cafasso learned that one of his convicts had been condemned to the forfeiture of his life, than he devoted a particular care to him. Not only did he hear his confession and give him Holy Communion, but he spoke so of life everlasting, that when the time for the fulfilling of the sentence was at last announced to the prisoner, he was just as ready to die as to live. Cafasso spent the last night with him, slept by his side, watched with him, prayed with him, said Mass for him on the last morning, gave Holy Viaticum and would willingly have died with him if it could have been for the salvation of his soul.[15]

Not all responded. Oftentimes the anger and frustration felt by the prisoner as he faced execution was directed at the priest. Some threatened him physically, one who was chained and could not raise a fist spit in his face. Cafasso met it all with gentleness.

14. Jalbert, *Walk While You Have the Light*, 128.

15. Jørgensen, *Don Bosco*, 81.

During the night before execution he would remain outside the cell of such an individual and occasionally remind the man that he was there, and praying for him.

As the approach of dawn brought fear the condemned would almost always reach out to Cafasso and the priest would respond. One violent criminal, chained to his cot, had long since lost contact with his childhood religion. Cafasso asked if he might place one more chain on him, and placed a "miraculous medal" about his neck. Under his blanket, the man attempted to move his hand to make a semblance of the sign of the cross. To his own surprise he remembered the words of the Hail Mary, "Holy Mary, mother of God, pray for us sinners now and at the hour of our death . . ."

Cafasso would often use the image of Mary, the mother of the executed criminal Jesus, to soften unrepentant men, oftentimes bringing in the image of the prisoner's own mother.

Refused entrance by one inmate, Cafasso assured him:

"Jesus and Mary suffered a great deal to have us, you and me, with them in Paradise. They know how much you suffer and they pity you. The sorrowful Madonna, our dear Mother, wishes you well and she can help you."

Cafasso moved away to a corner and quietly prayed. After a few minutes the man called out to him, saying, "Father, I'm ready to go to confession."[16]

Many went to death insisting on their innocence. To one such man who railed against his unjust sentence even as they approached the gallows, Cafasso said, "Sh! Be quiet. All the better for you if you are innocent. Even Our Blessed Lord was put to death though innocent."

To another who was wasting his last moments on earth by uselessly haranguing the crowds who had gathered for the spectacle of his death, Cafasso said, "My good man, Our Lord is waiting for you. Why talk longer with men?"

Cafasso did his best to protect the condemned from being a show for the common mob. While they would be riding in the cart on the way to the place of execution the prisoner, with his

16. Jalbert, *Walk While You Have the Light*, 144.

hands bound would be unable to hide his face from view. Cafasso would often hold a holy card up in front of his eyes affording at least a shred of privacy.

At the opposite extreme of those who died claiming innocence were the condemned who acknowledged their guilt so strongly they despaired about salvation. Cafasso was so confident of their immediate salvation that he began asking them while they were being readied to leave this earth to intercede for him that very day when they were in paradise with Christ. The last words of one such messenger, spoken to Cafasso, were, "I'm going to do that errand for you."[17]

After one execution as Cafasso was descending the ladder from the scaffold, a rung broke underfoot and he crashed to the ground. The gathered crowd, who had by this time popularized the "gallows priest" as a saint, immediately cried out in rage against the carelessness of the executioners. To protect them, Cafasso, regardless of how great an injury might have been afflicted on his already twisted spine, scrambled to his feet, assuring everyone that he was quite alright.

His concern for the executioners was not a momentary response. He saw them in their terrible role as needing his ministry as much as did the condemned. These people, along with their families, bore the odd and conflicting vengeance of people who wanted criminals off the streets and at the same time scorned these officers because of their official jobs.[18]

Cafasso was sensitive to this and these families appreciated and loved him for it. On one occasion, though he never allowed a moment for socializing, he wished to see one of the executioners and stopped at the man's house. He was not in and the man's wife asked him to join her for a cup of coffee. He declined the offer as he always did. The woman was hurt and accused him of refusing because of her husband's job, whereupon Cafasso, embarrassed by

---

17. Jalbert, *Walk While You Have the Light*, 150.

18. Jørgensen, *Don Bosco*, 82.

his insensitivity, remained in her kitchen, sharing one and then another cup of coffee with her.[19]

In one instance, Cafasso was offered the opportunity to act as the executioner. A much celebrated military prisoner, General Jerome Ramorino, who was to be executed for insubordination in battle, had asked that Cafasso be allowed to give the firing squad its orders to shoot. Cafasso refused to take on this role. But his emotional attachment to the young general and the stress involved in his accompanying him to his death, recorded in detail because of the great notoriety of the case, show why Cafasso died at a young age, burdened by so much of what he experienced.

Reflecting the anticlerical tone of the era, the disgraced officer had greeted the first arrival of Cafasso in his room by saying:

"My present state has no need of this further humiliation."

Accustomed to initial rejection, Cafasso kept calling upon him. Friendship grew. Ramorino asked the priest to read over the final letter that he wrote to his mother and presented his gold watch to him to give to her after his execution. Wishing to preserve his military image before the crowd who would assemble to watch his execution, he had received permission to march in a dignified cadence to the place of execution. When Cafasso, with his physical disabilities, fell behind, the general accepted the greater dignity of kindness and slowed his pace so that the priest could walk at his side. As they approached the place where he was to be shot, Cafasso suggested to him that, in that age when religion was ridiculed by the public authorities, an expression of faith spoken by him to the crowd would be good.

"One word from you," he said, "would be worth more than a hundred from us."

The words which he spoke were actions. He took the cross that Cafasso carried and reverently kissed it, eliciting applause from the crowd. As he was to take his place before the rifles he knelt to receive final absolution from Cafasso.

Although it was the practice of Cafasso to unite himself as best as he could to each convict, it was observed on this occasion

19. Jalbert, *Walk While You Have the Light*, 151.

that, as the squad was ordered to fire and the shots rang out, he averted his face from the scene.[20]

Saints Bosco and Cafasso

Because their lives are so intertwined and because Saint John Bosco is so much more known than Saint Joseph Cafasso, the relationship between the two and the comparison of their work is worthy of note.

John Bosco was twelve years old and Joseph Cafasso still a seminarian when the two first met. Cafasso, in his seminarian's cassock, was present at a parish festival in John's hometown where the boy watched him and became immediately smitten with hero worship. Ebullient as always, he approached Cafasso and offered to show him about, and in doing so he began their life long older, younger brother relationship. Bosco served at the altar at Cafasso's first Mass and followed in his footsteps toward priesthood.

Whereas Cafasso was shy of social involvements, Bosco, as a student, formed a social club he called the "Societa dell'Allegria"—"the Cheerful Group." During his years in the seminary he encountered professors who wore a forbidding demeanor and refused to mix with their students. It was a happy balance for him to have Joseph Cafasso not only as a friend but as professor and rector, for if the man was a shy workaholic, his love for others was evident to all and he was the most approachable to both women and men. His gentle philosophy was taught to the fledgling priests in his care and this philosophy was carefully recorded by Bosco, who became Cafasso's first biographer: "Jesus Christ, the infinite wisdom, used the words and idioms that were in use among those whom he addressed," Cafasso as rector advised them. When Bosco himself didn't catch the full meaning of this, Cafasso, who knew him and his family so well, gently suggested that he rewrite a sermon and

---

20. Jalbert, *Walk While You Have the Light*, 152–54.

in doing so "write so that your mother, who has no education, can understand you."[21]

Given his happy personality, John loved children, who, as he wrote, "form the most attractive portion of human society and in whom are centered all our hopes for a happy future." Children immediately returned his affection, and Cafasso astutely placed him in charge of the college's catechetical programs. Bosco, who had become sick at the foot of the scaffold, was less successful in the oppressive atmosphere of the prisons and was ill suited to share in Cafasso's rounds of the tiers. Jails and prisons, then as now, held children still in their formative years. Then, as now, idleness and lessons from more experienced inmates on how to commit crimes more effectively became their formation. Bosco asked Cafasso:

"If these boys had a friend who had some place to care for them and to assist and instruct them in their religion on feast days, would it not be possible to keep them from ruin, and at least lessen the number of those who returned to prison?"[22]

Cafasso encouraged Bosco to follow through on his ideas and allowed him to begin his first gatherings of street urchins in the college's courtyard. With the providential help of an inheritance willed to Cafasso, a house was bought and John Bosco's great life's work was begun. Childlike with children, he was childlike in his handling of finances as well, and until his own death Cafasso constantly worked at hauling his friend out of debt and seeing that his bills were eventually paid.

Feeding upon the love of his adopted children, John Bosco remained youthful into old age and lived a life that spanned from the Napoleonic Era almost until the twentieth century. Cafasso, who took upon himself the burdens of those who lived on the edge of despair, died under the weight of this, dying in early middle life. In his will he directed that a symbolic sum of money be given to each of the inmates in the prisons around Turin.[23]

---

21. Jalbert, *Walk While You Have the Light*, 31.
22. Phelan, *Don Bosco*, 67.
23. Phelan, *Don Bosco*, 67.

The twentieth-century church piously took to Saint John Bosco. Scores of churches and institutions for the young have been named after him, and Don Bosco stories of success with youths have been held up as a model of what should be done for the young. There is no corresponding rush to name anything after Saint Joseph Cafasso. He is the flip side of the Don Bosco stories of success with young people.

Saint Joseph Cafasso reminds us that there are a lot of these young people who fall through the cracks and who continue to live in darkness. But his life reminds us that the Christian community can never give up its charge to defend and protect these children to fullness of life.

Shocked by God's Grace

In 1987 several "Shock prisons" were opened in New York State, and for several years I ministered at one of them while keeping a foot in another facility that did little more than simply incarcerate. "Shock" is more like a military boot camp run according to the twelve-step program. Young male and female inmates are housed in well-separated squad bays. The only program that women and men share together are religious services, and gender separation was supervised by corrections officers.

This six-month program is open to non-violent offenders who have never been in the program before and whose sentence is no longer than four years. I tell inmates that the program is the best deal in the system.

Each day there is a schedule of controlled exercise, military-style drills, mandatory schooling, and interactive meetings from the moment they are rousted out of bed at 5 a.m. for a pre-breakfast run until they fall back into it exhausted at day's end.

In the school, communal responsibility for assignments means that an entire platoon is penalized for the failure of individual students to keep up with the work. Thus, in the dorms at night, where there is no television or radio to distract, it is not an unusual sight to see groups of inmates earnestly tutoring a slower classmate.

A majority of all these young inmates who are involved in Shock are incarcerated owing to drug- and alcohol-related incidents. Thus, the very backbone of the program is an attempt, through group counseling sessions, to bring these youngsters to a true assessment of themselves, what got them to where they are, and to their true potential for the future. The twelve-step program, used by both Alcoholics and Narcotics Anonymous, is called by some the greatest contribution to spirituality of the past century. This is the method employed as the basis for self-realization.

As well, every single day for an hour, each squad bay has a self-conducted community meeting to evaluate how they are doing as a group and as individuals. The officer present interrupts only if there is a mistake in procedures. Direct confrontations are never allowed. Instead, examples of failures are brought up, phrased in the third person (e.g. "What inmate is responsible for taking too much time with the iron and using it for clothes that aren't military garb?"—"What inmate is using offensive language?"). Those who recognize themselves in the accusation are to stand. Then, anyone who wishes to do so may then give a "teaching" as to how such behavior may be remedied. Again, this cannot be directed toward another inmate in the second person. The teaching must be in the first person: "What I find in myself that helps me correct such a fault is . . ."

A couple of examples. At one community meeting a young man stood and asked: "What inmate likes to go around the squad pulling on his crotch and saying, 'bang, bang'?" A long couple of minutes passed before one youngster finally stood up in tight-lipped embarrassment. The teachings of his peers were hard hitting:

"I would wonder if I was doing that, would I do it in front of Ms. Burke [the facility superintendent] if she came into the squad bay?"

"I would think that if I were doing that I would be having doubts about my own manhood. I would think that I had to resolve them without making a show of myself."

The inmate who was guilty of this action finally murmured that the lesson that he had learned from this was that this was unacceptable behavior.

When he sat down and the group went on to other matters, I noticed him quietly and as unobtrusively as possible reach up to brush away a tear which had slipped from the side of one eye. It had been a soul-searing moment of confrontation for him—far more dramatic than any undisciplined fist fight on an ordinary prison tier could ever had been. The great difference is that on an ordinary tier he might have won in a physical confrontation and been reinforced in his sexual macho stance. In this setting he had been made to see his own actions as they appear to others.

In a squad bay of woman inmates I witnessed a like "regress" in which the query was put forth, "What inmate got three write-ups at today's work duty for losing her temper and swearing at others?"

The guilty party stood while lessons were articulated. When it was time for her to state what she had learned she began by saying:

"The reason I was angry was because . . ."

The others interrupted in a chorus of voices, as would those at any twelve-step meeting:

"That's justifying."

She was determined to make known her reasons, each time interrupted by the calm but insistent chorus:

"That's justifying."

Finally after a long silence while she wrestled within herself she calmly said:

"I've got to learn not to take my temper out on other people."

It was a wonderful moment of self-realization. So too are moments in such meetings with women and sometimes men when they realize that on the streets:

"I don't have to let myself be used like that . . ."

Meetings focus on progress as well as regress. I witnessed a "progress" in which one inmate asked:

"What inmate got their first A today in school?"

When the culprit of earning a first A stood the whole platoon broke into hearty applause. Again I watched tears, this time of happy pride, come to the culprit's eyes, and I thought to myself, "I wouldn't be surprised if this is the first positive feedback this kid has ever received in life."

The positive and energized communal atmosphere flows over into religious services at these camps. No congregation I have experienced elsewhere compares with it. The responses are sharply pronounced and total; no murmured whispers or stone-faced participants allowed ("The Lord be with you"—"And with your spirit!"). The singing all but blows the front wall apart from the energy they put into hymns. This has spoiled me. After celebrating Mass in this context and then returning to church to preside over typical parish liturgies I do so wondering if the great majority of the congregation might not be overdosing on Valium.

Inmates are released from Shock not individually but in platoons after completing the six-month program. Thus, the release is aptly called a graduation. Inmates' families are invited to participate, and since the inmates are so young the atmosphere is not unlike that of a school commencement.

At one graduation, as the families and inmates were departing, an officer turned to me after posing while an inmate took a picture of him with his mother. He shook his head and said to me with a laugh:

"I've been working in prisons for twenty years. And if anyone had ever told me, before being in this program, that an inmate would take a picture of me with his mother as he was getting out, I wouldn't have believed it."

It said everything about the positive atmosphere engendered at the camp—and how young offenders can be saved from getting locked into a life of self-destruction.

Chapter 8

The Children Martyrs of Uganda[1]

IT IS A HUMILIATION for me as a jail chaplain to relate one aspect of the story of the 1886 martyrdom of the royal page boys of Baganda (present day Uganda). The clergymen who should have strengthened and supported them while they were in prison did not do so. They were afraid for their own safety. It is a reminder to us who serve as chaplains that we are not always present to the prisoners who have the most need of us. Oftentimes prisoners must minister to one another because of our absence or neglect. In the latter part of the nineteenth century, land-locked Boganda was an arena of competition between three religious groups: Muslims, Anglicans, and Roman Catholics. It is important to keep in mind that these religions, as brought to the Bogandans,

---

1. Much of the material from this chapter was drawn from Faupel, *African Holocaust*. Faupel notes in the introduction, "It is to be hoped that the patience of the non-African reader will not be too sorely tried by the biographical details of clans and relationships which are of considerable interest to Africans and to those who know the continent. It would indeed be tragic if any reader were to allow himself to be discouraged by these and fail to continue with the story of courage and achievement which, however inadequately it may be told, can hardly fail to thrill" (Faupel, *African Holocaust*, xi–xii).

were enmeshed with the colonial imperial policies of the British, the French, and Arab nations.[2]

The interests of both church and state were never separated in the midst of missionary endeavors, and Bogandan rulers might well have seen a growing threat to their independence with the arrival of each new missionary. The head of the Protestant mission, Rev. Alexander Mackay, could write after one royal attack upon his church members: "It was not a case of religious persecution pure and simple. It was a burst of fury against the Englishmen and any who consorted with them."[3] Baganda's kabaka (king) Mwanga was quoted as saying, "The English have come; they have built a fort. They eat my land."[4] This new age of modern colonialism was often noted as the "scramble for Africa."

Kabaka Mwanga

In the mid-1880s the newly-crowned Kabaka Mwanga was barely out of his teens, having inherited the throne at the death of his father. Impressive in appearance, he was, nonetheless, unstable in temperament and addicted to drugs. He changed policies with his chimerical moods, favoring one foreign group, then suddenly and repeatedly shifting that favor to another. If in other aspects of government he had shown himself to be an astute ruler one might suggest that he was shrewdly playing each competing group off the others. His entire administration, however, was dictated by his adolescent desires and emotional outbursts.

The French Catholic mission, led by Father Simeon Lourdel, arrived in 1879, two years after the Anglicans. The two groups of missionaries, reflecting the era in which they lived, viewed one another as representatives of heretical churches, much to the confusion of the people of Boganda, who had to disentangle such sentiments from the idea that both groups, believing in Jesus of

---

2. Islam arrived in the Middle Ages through the trade routes of Arabian nations.

3. Faupel, *African Holocaust*, 74.

4. "Mwanga II of Buganda."

Nazareth, loved not only God but their neighbor as well, including, presumably, neighbors who belonged to heretical groups of fellow Christians.

For the greater part of a decade, the two groups, competing with one another, somehow managed to establish a strong, continually growing Christian community. The only unity the missionaries showed was in their shared opposition to Islam. Mwanga, for a time, attempted to play these two foreign influences against one another. But his growing resentment toward the confines of Christian morality led him to the conclusion that both Catholic and Protestant groups were the enemy.

The Roman and Anglo Catholic Pages

Many of the royal pages had become Christians and actively preached their faith to newly appointed pages. Mwanga had been using the pages as objects for sexual pleasure. Becoming Christians, the boys drew courage from one another and refused to let him touch them. Mwanga festered in resentment to this dictation of morality by outsiders and underlings. Advisers who swayed him toward Islam warned him that the British, using Christianity as a front, would remove him from the throne and replace him with a woman ruler in imitation of their own Queen Victoria.

In January 1885 he suddenly lashed out against the Protestant mission, arresting several young men who were closely attached to Reverend Mackay. As they were led away, a young man named Mujosa, the kabaka's commander of forces and executioner, jeered at them saying: "You believe you will rise from the dead? Well, I shall burn you and see if it be so."

One of the boys blocked out his taunts by singing the hymn, "Daily, Daily, Sing the Praises." Encouraged by this, the others joined in with him. Three of the boys were then set aside for immediate execution. Mujosa had their arms hacked off. They were then tied to a scaffold and a pyre of wood built under them. They were burned to death.

An uneasy calm ensued for several months. Then the Anglican bishop, James Hannington arrived in Bogandan territory. He was arrested and held at a village a great distance from the Protestant mission, incarcerated in a hut which had been abandoned for so long it had been taken over by spiders and was filled with webs.

The bishop, having no idea of what was in store for him, pleaded for the mercy of being held in another hut. He was moved as he requested, but after several more days of imprisonment he was suddenly dragged outside and speared to death.

In that same month, Mwanga turned against his Christian majordomo, twenty-five-year-old Joseph Balikuddembe, suddenly pointing to him and announcing to his court:

"This is the fellow who always wanted to teach me and told me to put away my charms."

In the already tense atmosphere Balikuddembe had anticipated such an attack. He calmly responded:

"I am then to die for my religion."

"Do not let him live through the night," Mwanga commanded.

Despite an order that he be burned to death, the man charged with carrying out the order sympathized with Balikuddembe. As an act of kindness he beheaded the majordomo before lighting the fire.

Another fire, of accidental origin, intensified the crisis situation.[5] Adding to this setback, a military force sent by Mwanga against a neighboring nation was defeated. Frustrated by all of this, the kabaka directed his anger against the faction which had thwarted both his political power and his pursuit of sexual pleasures.

"I am tired of these Christians," he announced, "I will have them all put to death."

The final explosion of his wrath came in May of that year. Calling for a page while hunting and finding none because they were all at religious instruction, he exploded. The first Christian page brought before him, a sixteen-year-old, was beaten by Mwanga with a spear until it broke in his hands. Ordering the boy to be jailed until he should be beheaded, he seized two other pages and

5. In February of 1886, almost all of the royal enclosure was destroyed by flames which swept through the light wooden buildings.

ordered that they be immediately castrated. One of the boys died as the grotesque act of savagery was carried out.

At this point twenty-five-year-old Roman Catholic Charles Lwanga stepped forward to assume the moral leadership which Joseph Balikuddembe had exercised. He calmly informed the pages as to what they might expect from the kabaka.

"It seems likely that very shortly he will again order you to forsake your religion," he told them, "Then you have only to follow me in a body, and boldly affirm that you are Christians."[6]

When a frightened fourteen-year-old shuddered with fear, Lwanga gave him courage saying, "When the decisive moment arrives, I shall take your hand like this. If we have to die for Jesus, we shall die together hand in hand."

A Protestant youth, Mukasa, calmly affirmed to those around him, "We are going to be killed, but do not renounce your religion. Let us pray."

All the pages were called into the kabaka's presence where it was demanded of them whether or not they were Christians. In an amazing show of solidarity, none flinched. All of them, Catholic and Protestant, stepped forward to profess that they were, knowing that to do so meant death. A palace guard, Bruno Serunkuma, witnessing this, left his post, joined the pages, and declared that he too believed in Jesus.

The kabaka's chancellor objected to this, saying, "Don't try to make us believe that you are one of them."

Adamantly, Serunkuma insisted, "Most certainly I am. Only I have received instructions at night so as to avoid vexing the kabaka and being troubled by you. Charles has been my instructor, model and protector, and I wish to die with him for Jesus. I have spoken."

There were more than forty young men standing before Mwanga. As he ordered them all to be put to death, he commissioned the father of one of the young men to be the executioner of

---

6. Rare photographs of Charles Lwanga remind us that this moment of time is recent, not ancient, history. He was a handsome young man, with the face of a born leader in the ongoing "scramble for Africa."

his own son. As the pages were being led off to Mukajanga Prison, the kabaka gleefully yelled after them:

"Go then! Hurry to your heavenly king. He has the fatted calf waiting for you!"

Hesitating Clergy

At this juncture, the Catholic and Protestant clergymen, in their separated missions, hesitated as to what course of action should be taken. During the days that followed, while the pages remained in prison, the missionaries wrangled between themselves as to whether they should act singly or together. Finally, they approached the kabaka timidly, offering him gifts, placating him, hoping to make him forget his anger. Subsequent criticism of their actions is affected by hindsight. They were in a tortuous position, and their abject stance might have worked to bring the young madman around. They tried to buy time. It had worked in the past and could have worked again. Tragically, this time it did not. The kabaka's chancellor informed them coldly, "We will not drive you away. Teach as many as you like. But as many as you teach we will kill."

Unhesitating Lwanga

Without any contact with the clergy, the jailed pages, young in years and young in their faith, were left to draw strength from one another. In this setting Charles Lwanga baptized five catechumens who were still being instructed in the faith. At last the condemned were tied to one another and led on a ten-mile trek to the place of their execution.

A number of the young men were butchered along the way. Some were hacked to death. One was tied, cut to make his blood flow, and made the food of savage dogs. Four young girls were caught while hiding to witness the death of one of the victims. Enraged by this violation of a strict prohibition, the executioner cut off the hands of two of the girls and gouged their eyes out. The other two were remanded to the kabaka's harem.

At the execution site the prisoners were rolled in water so that the ropes binding them would shrink and cut into their flesh. They were then placed in huts for the night. One of the pages who survived remembered later that they encouraged one another lest anyone flinch at the last moment:

"We talked of God and said to one another, 'First to offer one-self to do a good act and then to omit it is playing the coward. The day has come for us to make good our promise. Let us die bravely for the cause of God.'"

Irritated by this, the guards broke the prisoners apart and isolated them from one another. They were kept as such for a week.

Ascension Day

On Ascension Thursday, June 3, 1886, they were brought together again outside the hut prisons. To the anger and frustration of their keepers, the boys' spirits remained undaunted, and they greeted each emerging prisoner with congratulatory cries of "Well done, brave lad."

As the death pyres were prepared a younger page who would later provide an eyewitness account was pulled away to be inexplicably spared. One of the others, who was about to die, called to him, "My poor Kamyuba. You are going to miss the ren-dezvous in heaven."

Charles Lwanga, who had shown such strong leadership, was taken first, singled out for extreme torture in his execution. He was tied to a mat and a fire was built under his feet. He was burned slowly until his legs were charred and only his torso remained. He never gave in to pain; he never yelled, even when he was breathing his last gasps. He finally called out "Katanda" ("My God") and died.

The thirty-one who remained were brought forth to die. The father who had been commanded by Mwanga to kill his own son was granted the mercy, by the executioners, of clubbing his son to death instead of burning him. The others were tied together on a scaffold which was then torched into a holocaust.

Three years after the martyrdom of the pages, Mwanga was overthrown in a coup which placed his Muslim brother upon the throne. The onetime persecutor sought refuge with the Christian missionaries, and they, in an ironic move which perhaps could only be understood by those who had to live through the moment, joined together, Protestant and Catholic, to restore him to the throne. Given the prospects of his younger brother's rule, they decided that Mwanga, as bad as he was, was the best hope for stability.

The Unity of Martyrdom

Not long thereafter, renamed Uganda was placed firmly within the British sphere of influence. For a number of years the separate Christian missions continued to war with one another both theologically and even in physical fighting. But the unity in martyrdom of the Protestant and Catholic pages was an instance that signaled the dawn of the coming century's growing sense of need for Christian unity in faith and action.

In 1964 Pope Paul VI during the universal council called "Vatican II" canonized Charles Lwanga and his martyred companions as saints. Of these companion martyrs twenty-two were Catholic, twenty-three Protestant. Paul was in a delicate spotlight. Protestants don't officially canonize saints. To include these martyrs as one group, Paul said: "Nor do we wish to forget the others who, belonging to the Anglican Confession, confronted death in the name of Christ."

In 1969 Paul went on pilgrimage to Sub-Saharan Africa, the first reigning pope to go there, and went to the place where the martyrs died, Protestant and Catholic together. In the case of the Ugandan martyrs, neophytes in their faith, jailed and denied the support of their clergy, they became the leaders instead of those led. Hopefully, their natural espousing of true ecumenism will continue to lead us.

One survivor, a Protestant lad, James Miti, in describing why a Catholic blacksmith hid those of both denominations in his house during the incident, said simply, "During the persecution, there was no distinction of religion or denomination. We were all Christian whether one went to Mackay or Pere Lourdel for religious instruction. All Christian converts were one family, with two internal arbitrary divisions. We loved one another and wished one another well."

May it be so, inside and outside of prisons and all places of incarceration.

Chapter 9

Oscar Wilde

Out of the Depths

ONE SUNDAY WHILE I was giving a homily to my inmates I referred to Soren Kierkegaard's idea of a "leap into faith." I mentioned his name, adding that he was a German philosopher. As I continued preaching I thought to myself, how foolish of me to bother saying Kierkegaard's name to a congregation who would neither know nor care anything about him. As the chapel emptied out after Mass, one of the men silently handed me a small piece of paper upon which was scrawled: "Soren Kierkegaard was a Dane."

It is a matter of both pride and prejudice to slip into the presumption that prisoners are unintelligent. People are not sent to jail because they failed an IQ test. Most inmates are, to begin with, street smart; from early childhood they have learned out of necessity to be survivors in a hard world unknown to the protected children of upper-middle-class suburbia.

Extraordinarily intelligent people, incarcerated poets, artistic and clever men and women, are oftentimes a threat to social workers, psychologists, and chaplains. We appear to them, oftentimes rightly, as dullard functionaries simply doing a job. After he was released from prison, Oscar Wilde wrote a poem, "The Ballad of Reading Jail," which he signed with his inmate appellation, C.C.3.

In it he referred to the prayers for the dead read by the chaplain to a man about to be hanged as being "the kiss of Caiaphas." Clarifying this for his editor, he said:

> By Caiaphas I do not mean the present chaplain of Reading; he is a good natured fool, one of the silliest of God's silly sheep; a typical clergyman in fact. I mean any priest of God who assists at the unjust and cruel punishments of man.[1]

Wilde, here, catches us chaplains on the hook of that which makes our position in the criminal justice system so hard to bear. We are caught in a no-win situation. As a chaplain I may disagree with all my soul with the death penalty and even to some uses of incarceration. Do I then show my protestation by refusing to be a part of it, thereby letting the prisoner die alone? Or, on the other hand, despising the role I play, should I walk with people to their executions offering to them, as Wilde calls it, "the kiss of Caiaphas?" Should I stand at the doorways of cells, feeling like "the silliest of God's silly sheep," attempting to console when consolation is impossible? How does a chaplain, born with less intelligence and perception than an Oscar Wilde, relate to people such as him when they are incarcerated? Wilde assesses us as a group, saying:

> They are of no help to any prisoner. Once every six weeks or so a key turns in the lock of one's cell door and the chaplain enters. One stands, of course, at attention. He asks if one has been reading the Bible. One answers "yes" or "no" as the case may be. He then quotes a few texts and goes out and locks the door. Sometimes he leaves a tract.[2]

Oscar Wilde, in turn, assessed himself immodestly but perceptively as:

> a man who stood in symbolic relation to the art and culture of my age . . . Few men hold such a position in their own lifetime and have it so acknowledged. It is usually discerned, if discerned at all, by the historian or the

1. Wilde, *Letters of Oscar Wilde*, 1070.
2. Wilde, *Letters of Oscar Wilde*, 1070.

critic, long after both the man and his age have passed away. With me it was different. I felt it myself and made others feel it.[3]

As a student at Oxford in the 1870s, he had won a reputation not altogether flattering for his outlandish behavior and dress and for his taste in decorating his room with peacock feathers. He became famous in society as a personality long before he earned a reputation as a writer.

In 1882 he went on a much-heralded tour of the United States, producing a play, *Vera*, while in New York. In Lincoln, Nebraska, after giving a lecture at the state university, it was suggested to him that he might like to see the state penitentiary. In a note that was pathetically ironic in light of what lay in his own future, the Victorian dandy wrote:

> They drove me out to see the great prison afterwards! Poor odd types of humanity in hideous, stupid dresses making bricks in the sun, and all mean looking, which consoled me, for I should hate to see a criminal with a noble face. Little whitewashed cells, so tragically tidy, but with books in them. In one I found a translation of Dante and Shelley. Strange and beautiful it seemed to me that the sorrow of a single Florentine in exile should, hundreds of years afterward, heighten the sorrow of some common prisoner in a modern jail, and one murderer with melancholy eyes to be hanged they told me in three weeks spending that interval in reading novels; a bad preparation for facing God or nothing. So every day I see something curious and new and now think of going to Japan.[4]

In the 1890s Wilde earned a solid reputation for greatness in the arts. He had published *The Picture of Dorian Gray*, and then produced the plays *Lady Windemere's Fan* and *Salome*, the latter for Sarah Bernhardt and produced in Paris when English censors refused to allow it on the London stage. He was married, had two sons, and was lionized by society. He was also involved

---

3. Wilde, *Letters of Oscar Wilde*, 1070.

4. Strugis, *Oscar Wilde*, 239.

in homosexual relationships with a number of young men, one of whom was Lord Alfred Douglas, son of the Marquis of Queensbury. Shortly after Wilde's greatest play, *The Importance of Being Earnest,* opened in 1895, Douglas, who professed a strong hatred for his father, pushed Wilde to sue him for libel after the marquis had made public insinuations about the play writer's relationship with his son.

Wilde, reluctant at first, gave in and took the marquis to court. It was an ill-advised move; homosexual conduct was a criminal act in nineteenth-century England. Lawyers brought forth evidence that proved that Wilde was guilty of such, and that he was, therefore, a corrupter of youths. The tables were dramatically turned. In May of 1895, Wilde the accuser stood as a convicted felon in the docket of the Old Bailey and received a sentence of two years imprisonment with hard labor. He was in a situation that would previously have been beyond his imagination; his entire existence suddenly became a nightmare.

For I Should Hate to See a Criminal with a Noble Face

Taken from court and moved from one jail to another by train, he stood on a station platform, in handcuffs, listening to the laughter of a gathered crowd for whom the sight of Oscar Wilde reduced to such a state was an object of great entertainment. Arriving at the prison, he was made to strip and to take a bath in water which had been used by a number of men before him. The whole process was such a shock to his physical and emotional system that it was days before he was able to eat anything.

In the dark months of loneliness in his cell he began to write a long epistle, published only after his death, entitled *De Profundis.*[5] It is a mixed bag of a document, perhaps because it reflects the swirl of moods to which a prison inmate is prey. Wilde is angry at young Alfred Douglas and at himself. And yet, amid the recriminations

5. Wilde, *Complete Works.* "De Profundis" is from the first line of Psalm 130 in Latin—"Out of the depths I have cried to you, Oh Lord."

and sometimes self-pity one reads a series of reflections written by a man trying to square himself with God. Befitting the title, he began his process at the depths, observing:

> Prison life, with its endless privation and restrictions makes one rebellious. The most terrible thing about it is not that it breaks one's heart, hearts are made to be broken, but that it turns one's heart to stone. One sometimes feels that it is only with a front of brass and a lip of scorn that one can get through the day at all. And he who is in a state of rebellion cannot receive grace, to use the phrase of which the church is so fond, so rightly fond I dare say for in life, as in art, the mood of rebellion closes up the channels of the soul and shuts out the airs of heaven.[6]

It is an interesting observation, for it flies in the face of the entire modern day-concept—and name—of the "penitentiary" as a rehabilitative experience for convicted offenders. And yet, even if imprisonment and a mood of rebellion threatened to turn Wilde's heart to stone, he made himself realize that he was responsible for his own fall. His description of this acceptance stands as a goad to conscience for every person of talent who has ever thrown away gifts of mind and spirit only to wallow in temporal and foolish pursuits. He wrote:

> I had genius, a distinguished, high social position, brilliancy, intellectual daring . . . Along with these things I had things that were different. I let myself be lured into long spells of senseless and sensual ease. I amused myself with being a flaneur, a dandy, a man of fashion, and surrounded myself with the smaller values and meaner minds. I became the spendthrift of my own genius, and to waste an eternal youth gave me a curious joy. Tired of being on the heights I deliberately went to the depths in search of new sensations. What the paradox was to me in the sphere of thought, perversity became to me in the sphere of passion. Desire, at the end, was a malady, or a madness, or both. I grew careless of the lives of others. I took pleasure where it pleased me and passed on. I forgot

6. Wilde, *Complete Works*, 1025.

that every little action of the common day makes or un-makes character, and that therefore what one has done in the secret chamber one has someday to cry aloud on the housetop. I ceased to be the lord over myself. I was no longer the captain of my soul, and did not know it . . . I ended in horrible disgrace. There is only one thing for me now, absolute humility.[7]

Abandoned by the society which once had crowned him with laurels, Wilde began to feel a sense of oneness with the society of captives with whom he now shared life. One day, during exercise in the yard, a fellow inmate whispered to him in a hoarse voice, "I am sorry for you. It is harder for the likes of you than it is for the likes of us."

Wilde felt tears spring to his eyes.

He managed to answer, "No, my friend, we all suffer alike."

He did not yet know how to whisper without making himself noticed and was punished for breaking the rule of silence. And yet, this moment of kindness helped him to realize something about the class of people for whom jails are a common reality of life. He was beginning to see:

> The poor are wiser, more charitable, more kind, more sensitive than we are. In their eyes prison is a tragedy in a man's life, a misfortune, a casualty, something that calls for sympathy in others. They speak of one who is in prison as of one who is "in trouble" simply. It is the phrase they always use, and the expression has the perfect wisdom of love in it. With people of our rank it is different. With us prison makes a man a pariah.[8]

Wilde's society friends deserted him and creditors encircled to plague him with bills that he could not pay. Once more, to the amusement of London society, he was brought in chains to court. On this occasion one of the effete young men who had surrounded and fawned after the author when he was at the height of glory showed himself to be a true friend. Robert Ross, who after Wilde's

7. Wilde, *Complete Works*, 1017.

8. Wilde, *Complete Works*, 1016.

death would valiantly manage to reclaim the royalty rights of Wilde's plays for the author's children, joined those who waited to catch a glimpse of the prisoner. After the incident, Wilde wrote:

> When I was brought down from my prison to the court of bankruptcy between two policemen Robbie waited in the long dreary corridor that before the whole crowd, whom an action so sweet and simple hushed into silence, he might gravely raise his hat to me, as handcuffed and with bowed head I passed him by. Men have gone to heaven for smaller things than that. It was in this spirit, and with this mode of love that the saints knelt down to wash the feet of the poor, or stooped to kiss the leper on the cheek. I have never said a single word to him about what he did. I do not know to the present moment whether he is aware that I was even conscious of his action. It is not a thing for which one can render formal thanks in formal words. I store it in the treasury house of my heart. I keep it there as a secret debt that I am glad to think I can never possibly repay.[9]

Oscar had said that prison turned one's heart to stone. He never changed in that opinion. And yet, the personal acts of kindness, the sharing of sorrows with others, opened his heart to the workings of grace, for, as Oscar himself decided, "Where there is sorrow, there is holy ground."[10] He felt himself drawn more and more to such holiness.

"At Christmas," he wrote, "I managed to get hold of a Greek Testament, and every morning, after I have cleaned my cell and polished my tins, I read a little of the Gospels, a dozen verses taken by chance anywhere. It is a delightful way of opening the day."[11]

He began not merely to read about Jesus but to feel drawn toward him. The once worldly artist became childlike in his sense of discovery. He observed:

---

9. Wilde, *Complete Works*, 1016.
10. Wilde, *Complete Works*, 1011.
11. Wilde, *Complete Works*, 1033.

Christ, like all fascinating personalities, had the power not merely of saying beautiful things himself, but of making other people say beautiful things to him; and I love the story St. Mark tells us about the Greek woman ... who, when as a trial of her faith he said to her that he could not give her the bread of the children of Israel, answered him that the "little dogs ... who are under the table eat of the crumbs that the children let fall ..." Pity he has, of course, for the poor, for those who are shut up in prisons, for the lowly, for the wretched, but he has far more pity for the rich, for the hard hedonists, for those who waste their freedom in becoming slaves to things.[12]

And of the mystery of redemption:

There is still something to me almost incredible in the idea of a young Galilean peasant imagining that he could bear on his own shoulders the burden of the entire world: all that had been already done and suffered, and all that was yet to be done and suffered: oppressed nationalities, factory children, thieves, people in prison, outcasts, those who are dumb under oppression and whose silence is heard only of God ... so that at the present moment all who come in contact with his personality ... find that the ugliness of their sins is taken away and the beauty of their sorrow revealed to them ...

Is there anything that for sheer simplicity of pathos wedded and made one with the sublimity of tragic effect can be said to equal or approach even the last act of Christ's passion, the little supper with his companions one of whom had already sold him for a price ... the coronation ceremony of sorrow, one of the most wonderful things in the whole of recorded time: the crucifixion of the Innocent One before the eyes of his mother and of the disciple whom he loved ...

One cannot but be grateful that the supreme office ["prayer"] of the Church should be the playing of the tragedy without the shedding of blood, the mystical presentation by means of dialogue and costume and gesture even of the Passion of her Lord, and it is always a source

12. Wilde, *Complete Works*, 1034.

of pleasure and awe to me to remember that the ultimate survival of the Greek Chorus, lost elsewhere to art, is to be found in the servitor answering the priest at Mass.[13]

Praxis

In the prison, Wilde began to reach into the lives of his fellow inmates. He became horrified at the uselessness of incarcerating teenagers in a limbo of non-activity, and from his own cell took up the activity of writing to newspapers to protest such "an outrage on humanity and common sense. It comes from stupidity." He argued, "If, however, they are sent to prison, during the day they should be in a workshop or a schoolroom with a warder. At night they should sleep in a dormitory, with a night warder to watch after them. They should be allowed exercise for at least three hours a day. The dark, badly ventilated, ill smelling prison cells are dreadful for a child, dreadful indeed for anyone. One is always breathing bad air in prison."[14]

Wilde also cried out in letters to the press about the treatment of the "insane or weak minded."[15]

"Each prison," he observed, "has its half witted clients who return again and again, and may be said to live in prison."[16] Toward the end of his own sentence, Wilde watched the treatment of "a wretched half witted lad who was flogged at doctors orders" and whose derangement "was being treated as if he were shamming." Wilde found himself drawn toward this particularly simple fellow with "his silly grin and idiotic laughter to himself and the peculiar restlessness of his eternally twitching hands."[17]

Oscar sat behind him in chapel and observed, "Sometimes he would bury his head in his hands, an offense against chapel

13. Wilde, *Letters of Oscar Wilde*, 1060–64.
14. Wilde, *Letters of Oscar Wilde*, 1064.
15. Wilde, *Letters of Oscar Wilde*, 1064.
16. Wilde, *Letters of Oscar Wilde*, 1064.
17. Wilde, *Letters of Oscar Wilde*, 1064.

regulations, and his head would be immediately struck by a warder so that he should keep his eyes fixed permanently in the direction of the Communion table. Sometimes he would cry, not making any disturbance but with tears streaming down his face and an hysterical throbbing in his throat."[18]

By now, Wilde had developed that sense of oneness with his fellow inmates exemplified by the heroic empathy of Cardinal Mindszenty. In an occurrence almost duplicate to that described by Mindszenty, Wilde recorded:

> On Saturday week last I was in my cell at about one o'clock occupied in cleaning and polishing the tins I had been using for dinner. Suddenly I was startled by the prison silence being broken by the most horrible and revolting shrieks, or rather howls, for at first I thought some animal like a bull or cow was being unskillfully slaughtered outside the prison walls. I soon realized, however, that the howls proceeded from the basement of the prison, and I knew that some wretched man was being flogged. I need not say how hideous and terrible it was for me, and I began to wonder who it was who was being punished in this revolting manner. Suddenly it dawned upon me that they might be flogging this unfortunate lunatic. My feelings on the subject need not be chronicled.[19]

Later, it was confirmed for Wilde by another prisoner that, as he suspected, "the howls that had horrified us all were his," and that he had been given twenty-four lashes. The next day, Wilde wrote:

> I saw the poor fellow at exercise, his weak ugly wretched face bloated by tears and hysteria almost beyond recognition. He walked in the center ring along with the old men, the beggars, and the lame people, so that I was able to observe him the whole time. It was my last Sunday in prison, a perfectly lovely day, the finest day we had had the whole year, and there, in the beautiful sunlight, walked this poor creature made once in the image of God, grinning like an ape, and making with his hands

18. Wilde, *Complete Works*, 1064.

19. Wilde, *Complete Works*, 1065.

the most fantastic gestures, as though he was playing in the air on some invisible stringed instrument, or arranging and dealing counters in some curious game. All the while these hysterical tears, without which none of us ever saw him, were making soiled runnels on his white swollen face.[20]

Rejection by the "Christian Community"

The day that Oscar Wilde was released from prison, a remnant of the onetime crowd of society friends who had paid him homage gathered at the home of a friend in London to welcome him back. He arrived and at first seemed less ill at ease than they. He joked with them, focusing his attention on one woman who was a fashion plate.

"Sphinx," he told her, "how marvelous of you to know exactly the right hat to wear at seven in the morning to meet a friend who has been away! You can't have got up, you must have sat up."[21]

He had sent off a request to a Roman Catholic house of retreat, asking that he might spend time there in order to get hold of himself before reentering the world. He was awaiting an immediate reply. As remembered by a man in the room, "The man returned with the letter. We all looked away while Oscar read it. They replied that they could not accept him in the retreat house at the impulse of the moment. It must be thought over for at least a year. In fact, they refused him. Then he broke down and sobbed bitterly."[22]

The rejection by the priests at the retreat house might be attributed to timidity. During Wilde's trial, when an Anglican priest, Rev. Stewart Headlam, had sympathetically posted bail for him, a mob threatened to stone the clergyman. To offer hospitality to a convicted homosexual was certainly to risk one's own reputation. The motivation for rejection, however, might have been stronger than simply timidity. The crime of which Oscar Wilde had been

20. Wilde, *Letters of Oscar Wilde*, 1060–65.

21. Sturges, *Oscar Wilde*, 585.

22. Sturges, *Oscar Wilde*, 585.

found guilty was one that raised loud and righteous cries of indignation from moralists. To stand with those who had stood ready to cast stones was then as now to stand in company with the "good people" of society.

Oscar had sorely needed help such as he had sought from the priests at the retreat house. He had left prison not rehabilitated but shattered.

"The prisoner looks to liberty," he reflected, "as an immediate return to all his ancient energy, quickened into more vital forces by long disuse. When he goes out he finds he still has to suffer. His punishment, as far as its effects go, lasts intellectually and physically, just as it lasts socially."[23]

Unrelenting Purgatory

Although he had looked forward to again writing plays, he never did so. The only works produced after his incarceration were the powerful *Ballad of Reading Gaol* and *De Profundis*. He only lived three more years; he lived them as a pariah, rejected by fellow believers who vocalized, with Wilde, faith in a forgiving Savior. He, in contrast, did not turn his back on the society of people he had come to know while incarcerated, feeling compelled to write to newspapers upon his release, taking up the cause of incarcerated children and the mentally ill.

At the same time, he excused himself from joining his friend, author Frank Harris, on a trip, apologizing that he was still too weakened from his imprisonment to be good company and that he did not want to diminish his friend's enjoyment.

Having admitted that he was of the social class of convicts, Wilde entered into a correspondence with Michael Davitt, a Fenian activist who served seven years behind bars and who was repeatedly violated from parole and reimprisoned owing to his constant political activities. Davitt had become interested in Wilde's public exposé of the deranged inmate being beaten at the doctor's orders.

23. Sturges, *Oscar Wilde*, 185–86.

One would like to write a happy ending to Wilde's story, to say that he found happiness, was welcomed into a sense of community by those who called themselves Christians, and developed into a leading moral crusader for prison reform over a long and fruitful career. However, Oscar had little prospects of knowing happiness if it depended upon Christian forgiveness being extended by Christians in name. He had sojourned to France because so few people were willing to open doors to him in England. He encountered rejection there as well.

Abandoned by others, he vacillated between abandoning himself to his former, self-destructive life of profligacy and his continuing hope to be accepted into a Christian community, specifically into the Roman Catholic Church. He traveled to Rome, where he visited Robert Ross, the young man who had raised his hat to the shackled Wilde when he was brought from prison to bankruptcy court.

Wilde was greatly impressed with Pope Leo XIII, frequently attending the pope's public audiences and being blessed by him on seven occasions.

Wilde asked Ross to introduce him to a priest who would formally receive him into the church. Ross demurred. He was still not convinced that Wilde was serious. Wilde himself was never quite sure that he was serious, either. Ross's refusal allowed Wilde to joke that "whenever I wanted to be a Catholic [Ross] stood at the door with a flaming sword barring the way."[24]

Returning to Paris, Wilde became seriously ill, sinking so quickly that those around him realized that he was in danger of death. Ross hurried to France by train and was horrified by his friend's condition. Forgetting his criteria about finding an intellectual enough theologian for Wilde, he rushed out into the streets to find the first available priest, returning with an Irish Passionist, Father Cuthbert Dunne. Oscar was received into the church and attempted to repeat with the priest the name of Jesus, the acts of Contrition, Faith, Hope, and Charity, with an act of resignation to the will of God.

24. Sturges, *Oscar Wilde*, 651.

He lived one more day. Father Dunne visited him again, and again they prayed together, the priest giving him absolution as he had done the day before. Oscar Wilde then left a world, which, for him, had become a world of rejection and fears of rejection, to be accepted by the infinite mercy of Christ.

Chapter 10

The Other Mother Seton

BURNOUT IS A GREAT problem for even the most dedicated of those who would minister to the incarcerated. The never ending sameness of inmate problems; the sameness of excuses for relapses and repeat offenses; the morass of despair which oftentimes would drown the rescuer along with those in need of rescuing. This reality of burnout, which is so often referred to as a danger for caregivers in the present day and age, was no less a danger for caregivers in the first year of the twentieth century when an inmate at Sing Sing Prison penned a loving tribute to a group of women, religious Sisters of Mercy, whose ministry to the inmates he had witnessed for "many years," and who consistently seemed to be beyond the touch of professional burnout:

> They always come lugging with them a huge box of dainties for the poor chaps in the hospital. Here are the questions they ask us: "How long must you serve?" Never, "What crime did you commit?" "Have you mother, sister, wife or children?—are they destitute? What can we do to help them?" You see, there is no more theorizing on their part than there is on ours. And their work does not cease with their offer. We do not like to speak of our difficulties to anybody outside of the sisters, and they never so much

as whisper of the aid they render. We love the sisters for
the good cheer they always bring to us, for the genuine
affection they give us and for their confidence in us.[1]

Midway through the century that had just ended, this ministry at Sing Sing had been initiated by Sister M. Catherine Seton
who had been born in 1800 and whose long life came just short
of spanning that century in its entirety. That she would have embraced a ministry to the incarcerated might have surprised those
who knew her only by her background, for she had been raised
in what might be termed a doubly sheltered environment. Her
mother, Elizabeth Seton, the first person born in the United States
who would be canonized a saint in the Catholic Church, was a
socially well-born widow who converted to Catholicism and then
decided to found what would be the United States' first women's
religious order, the Sisters of Charity.[2]

Funds to start this community were donated to Mrs. Seton by
a retired sea captain, Samuel Cooper, another convert to Catholicism, who providentially stipulated that she build her establishment
at Emmitsburg, Maryland, where she would be within proximity of
a budding university, Mount St. Mary's, founded by two remark-
able priests who had survived the French Revolution, Simon Brute
and John Dubois. Elizabeth's two sons were placed in the college.
Catherine, the only daughter to survive childhood, was raised in
the convent of sisters. The two French priests, especially the Napoleonic, strong-minded Dubois, added stability to the charisma of
Elizabeth Seton and stability to the lives of her fatherless children.

Brute, the younger of the two men, had been a boy during
the French Reign of Terror. As priests were arrested and sent to
the guillotine, Brute's iron-willed and gallant mother, while committing the capital offense of hiding priests in her own house, sent
her young son to witness and report upon the trials and executions
of others. The memory of all this was seared into his soul. In later

---

1. Anonymous, "A Prisoner's Tribute."

2. Much of the material in this chapter comes from Shaw, *John Dubois:
Founding Father.*

years he related it to the students and sisters in Emmitsburg and finally committed it to writing.

Catherine was raised on these stories, including Brute's account of how he would slip into the prisons of the revolution "disguised as a baker's boy and carrying a big bread basket on my head," accompanying a priest disguised as a baker who was clandestinely bringing Holy Communion to the inmates.

John Dubois, a schoolmate of Maximilian de Robespierre and Camille Desmoulins, spent his first years of priesthood ministering inside of an institution for the insane, working along with the Daughters of Charity in Paris. The first rule of Elizabeth Seton's order, preserved in their archives in Emmitsburg, is in John Dubois's handwriting and is adapted from the rule of the order with whom he had served. He escaped from Paris shortly before the infamous "September Massacre" of priests and made his way across the Atlantic to Virginia, where he worked for almost a full generation of time on horseback, serving far-settled Catholics, before establishing his college at Emmitsburg.

Keen to the politicized injustices of legal systems, Dubois once wrote an impassioned letter to Governor James Monroe of Virginia, pleading for the life of a slave sentenced to be hanged for killing a master who had cheated him out of two hundred dollars when it had been agreed that this sum, freely earned by the slave, would purchase his freedom. Dubois demanded of the American revolutionary icon Monroe "whether the law has a right to punish a murder committed in defense of a right which no one could lawfully rob him of."[3]

As doubly sheltered as Catherine's childhood environment of social class and cloister might otherwise have been, she was educated by these men who had personally experienced so much of life's raw cruelties.

"When you come again to the Mount," Dubois advised the young girl, "you will pick out of my library what may suit you. Meanwhile I send you the dreadful *Expedition to Russia*. See what

---

3. Shaw, *John Dubois*, 31.

ambition can undergo for this world. Oh if we could do half of it for heaven, how rich we would be."[4]

He was very much her spiritual father. The two would exchange gifts as well as books. She would embroider him a stole. He in return would send to the convent a preserved pineapple, orange, and two green apples, playfully advising her:

"In the choice, believe me, take the smallest."[5]

Catherine was twenty when her mother died, and her inclination was to formally join her mother's community as a sister. Wisely, John Dubois would not let her. Arranging for her to live with a wealthy family who were friends of her mother, he told her that she had to experience the world outside lest "[you] one day might form to yourself a false picture of the world and regret a shadow because you would think it a reality."[6]

After he pushed her into the world she traveled extensively in Europe, learning that she was adept at quickly picking up other languages. She then came back to New York City, where Dubois had become bishop, and there lived with the family of her socially well-married brother William. When Dubois died in 1842 she was with him and closed his eyes. Shortly afterwards she, having had her interim of experiencing a salon's view of the world, formally entered the convent.

She did not join the community founded by her mother. The move for the canonization of Elizabeth Seton had already begun and the celebrity status grafted onto Catherine because of this was intimidating.

An Irish community called Sisters of Mercy and dedicated to working with the poor had newly arrived in the States. She became their first American novice. A year after her entry, and just as she was becoming fully professed, New York's Charity Commissioners

4. Shaw, *John Dubois*, 80. (John Dubois to Catherine Seton, December 26, 1818. Archives at St. Mary's College, Emmitsburg, MD.)

5. Shaw, *John Dubois*, 80. (John Dubois to Catherine Seton, December 26, 1818. Archives at St. Mary's College, Emmitsburg, MD.)

6. Shaw, *John Dubois*, 90. (John Dubois to Catherine Seton, December 26, 1818. Archives at St. Mary's College, Emmitsburg, MD.)

invited the sisters to make visitations at the city's almshouses, hospitals, the metropolitan jail (aptly called "the Tombs") and Sing Sing prison. The sheltered and aristocratic Sister Catherine volunteered to take charge of the ministry to the imprisoned.

We don't know much about the day-to-day details of the ministry of these Sisters of Mercy. They weren't angling to win a testimonial banquet. As the above Sing Sing inmate observed, they worked with "never so much as [a] whisper of the aid they render," content to let God keep record of their labors. The self-effacing glimpses we have of their work come from in-house convent memoirs about individual sisters' personalities kept only for the sake of love and community enjoyment.

The remembrances about Sister Catherine Seton give happy proof that once she entered into prison chaplaincy she not only remained devoted to it for the rest of her life; she did so with an ever-fresh, ever-lighthearted nonjudgmental openness towards the inmates she visited. Ministering at the Tombs and at Sing Sing, moving along each tier, talking with inmates cell by cell, required standing on her feet all day on concrete floors. She always waved away any suggestion that the task ever left her weary or footsore.

"It is my privilege," she would insist. Already fluent in French and Italian from her European sojourns, she learned Spanish and German so that she could communicate with more of the immigrant inmates.

At the time of her death, a newspaper would write of her that "No one probably ever acquired such influence and control over the thieves and robber class of New York." Such men, the writer observed, "came to her for years to seek advice and guidance, they endeavored to make her the trustee for their wives and children, so implicit was their confidence in her."[7]

Because Sister Catherine never turned her back on those who she loved throughout all her life, the paper could also relate that a sometimes odd traffic jam could occur when "she would be called to the convent parlor to meet at the same time some relative

---

7. Gallagher, "Catherine Josephine Seton," 111.

moving in the best circles, and perhaps some unfortunate whose steps to the convent door had been followed by a detective."[8]

She wouldn't allow these friends from "the best circles"—or for that matter anyone else—to lionize her for living her life with those from other than the best circles.

People within her proximity seem consistently to have been attracted to her personality, going back so far as to when she was a fledgling teacher in the school run by her own mother. She was never a "heavy duty" person even when times and settings were such. Already in her sixties during the Civil War and remaining with her prison ministry in New York while others of the sisters traveled southward to serve in military hospitals, she wrote to her dearest friend, Mother Augustine, superior of the nursing sisters, encouraging her by saying, "My spirit hovers near you as you go your rounds of blessed care for the wounded and the suffering . . . How you must be filled with holy thoughts and deep love when you see bloody limbs and crushed humanity."[9] Perhaps owing to the fact that she already knew that the sisters had arrived at the military hospital to find the place so inhumanely filthy that they had to scrub down even the blood-splattered walls before doing anything else, she wryly addressed her letter to "Darling Mother Augustine—Chief cook and bottle washer, Beaufort, NC." Assessing of her friend's labors: "I suspect you will turn out to be a second St. Catherine of Genoa and we will have to beatify you at least." Of her own ministry to "crushed humanity" she simply mentions in passing: "We have come bravely through the summer. I was able to go to the Prison every Wednesday and Sunday but one, when I was a little too weak to go."

Her direct innocence could disarm even the most manipulative of jailhouse opportunists. Once when she was bringing clothes to an inmate the trousers to the suit slipped out of the package and fell without her notice to the floor. As she reached the cell of the prisoner who had requested the clothes, she realized the loss and,

8. Gallagher, "Catherine Josephine Seton," 111.

9. Mother Catherine to Mother Augustine McKenna. Undated. Sisters of Mercy archives, Dobbs Ferry, New York.

turning to see an inmate down the tier busily raking them into his cell, she gently called that the trousers were part of the package being brought to another man. He quickly said he was just picking them up for her.

The raking in of those trousers is the sort of immediate gratification opportunism that can cause caregivers to become jaded about those to whom they minister and take to generalizing as to what "they" are "always up to." Catherine Seton, year in and year out, decade in and decade out, unfailingly continued to see all of these men as her "darling souls."

On special celebrations the sisters with whom she lived knew how to send her the very best as gifts: clothes for her inmates. On her twenty-fifth anniversary she was overjoyed with the community's presentation to her: several suits for men who would be released, each suit with a sum of money carefully sewn into the jacket pocket.

A paragraph from the community annals records one such party, capturing for us the lighthearted air of Catherine's "hilaritas" with which this carried on, and this after a point at which Catherine was serving as a senior authority in the community and addressed as "Mother."

On one of her feast days the novices presented her with a large basket of clothes of all sizes and kinds. "Is it all for my poor?" she cried like a delighted child. One young nun drew out of it a shoe. Mother Catherine laughingly said: "Oh, dear, get me the mate to that, as all my men have two feet, thank God."

As the young donors drew out piece after piece of clothing they would say: "Here, Mother, is a hat for you!" "I need it, darling, for a man."—"Here is a coat for you." "I have just the man it will fit," and so on all through the contents of the big receptacle. It would be hard to determine which was the more pleased at the gift, the unselfish Mother or the young novices who had bestowed it.

Another trunk arrived at the convent one day, shipped from Philadelphia and addressed to Mother Catherine. The immediate assumption was that it contained items for the prison ministry. The sisters could not get it opened until they forced the lock. Instead of clothing or books they found it filled with weapons, jimmies, and assorted burglary tools. Amid the surprise and laughter Catherine surmised that the trunk had been sent by a particular ex-convict and was assured that she was right in her surmising when she learned not long afterwards of his death. He had wanted to get rid of the tools of his trade before facing God, and knew the safest person to whom he could bequeath them.

Catherine walked with many a man who was getting ready to face God. For all the years that she visited Sing Sing she ministered to those who were sentenced to be executed, remaining with them as long as the prison rules allowed her. She would accompany them to chapel for the last time, where the condemned were allowed to receive Holy Communion, and then, forbidden to attend at the gallows, she would remain in chapel before the Blessed Sacrament praying for the man until he was in eternity.

The beautiful reality of grace is that none of this discouraged her, none of it left her own soul hardened or jaded. The archives of the Sisters include Catherine's handwritten meditations. Many of them are on Christ's own sufferings. In one entry she reflects upon Jesus being troubled in spirit when, at the Last Supper, he must acknowledge to his apostles that "one of you will betray me" (Matt 26:21). It was enough to afflict this dear shepherd who would leave the ninety-nine in the wilderness to rescue one stray sheep. (Matt 18:12–13).

Only when she was well into old age did she reluctantly agree that she could no longer walk the jail and prison tiers. Still, she fought taking to the easy chair. It was her duty to recruit and educate the young novices into prison ministry. When some shrank from the task, she would encourage them with the sufferings of Christ. If true innocence means that one be fully exposed to evil and yet remain unaffected by it, Mother Catherine Seton, who for so many decades was immersed in the darkest realms of the effects of evil, is a joyous example of that innocence. The case may be easily made that she be canonized as a saint, as was her mother.

On a professional and practical level, she stands as a grace-filled and lighthearted inspiration for all who minister to prisoners and who feel themselves succumbing to the professional danger of "burnout."

It is not a route one has to take.

Chapter 11

Charles Colson

Re-upping for Prison

CHARLES COLSON MIGHT NOT have an immediate credibility among some Americans who remember him as a major figure in the Watergate scandal of Richard Nixon's presidency. Those who know as well that he became a "born-again Christian" lay preacher might not feel that this of itself justifies any greater cause for faith in him owing to the great scandals in recent history involving well-known television evangelists. An interviewer in a *Publishers Weekly* article about Colson noted his Washington reputation for being a cynic and decided that he "still is, though to a lesser degree." Listening to him witness to his faith as a Christian, the interviewer bluntly challenged him:

"Why should anyone believe you?"[1]

And yet, the interviewer was being no more harsh than Colson himself in describing his own life and his early, burning ambitions. As a young marine lieutenant on military maneuvers in Puerto Rico he went to extremes to prove that he was tough. Although there was a standing order that local residents were not to enter military areas and that military personnel were not to purchase contraband from them, the order was ordinarily winked at.

1. Fields, "PW Interviews," 117.

On a hot July day while Colson was leading his men on maneuvers they encountered an old man who Colson described as "leading a scrawny donkey nearly collapsing under the load of two huge, obviously ice-filled canvas sacks."

The aggressive lieutenant ordered his sergeant to arrest the elderly man "whose smile suddenly turned to stone." The chilled fruit juice he had brought to sell was yanked from the sacks of ice and tossed to the cheering marines. Colson would one day ruefully remember:

"The old man squinted at me with doleful eyes. I had not given a fleeting thought to the fact those satchels of juice might have represented the old man's life savings or that my order could mean an entire family might go hungry for months."

All that mattered to him at the moment was that "I had proven I was tough."

At a more mature stage of development, this man, who had joined in the making of policy for the United States government, could conclude of this incident of Yankee chauvinism, "Small wonder that years later 'independence' movements in Puerto Rico agitated for removal of the United States military."[2]

He became a lawyer and decided that "the most desirable clients were those able to pay the most." Hobnobbing almost exclusively with "corporate executives or individuals with resources," he recorded, with no little sense of irony, "my only brush with criminal law or the poor or disadvantaged were those dreaded occasions—once or twice a year at most—when my number was called in one of the local courts and I was assigned to an indigent client. Ultimately, of course, I saw justice as the instrument for removing from society and punishing those who refused or were unable to live by the rules people like myself made."[3]

His personal life took a back seat to his ambitions. His first marriage ended in divorce. Nevertheless he had made a name for himself in the world of politics and in 1969 when newly elected Richard Nixon put together his White House staff he invited

2. Colson, *Loving God*, 101.

3. Colson, *Loving God*, 169–70.

Colson to be a part of it. In this capacity he quickly earned a reputation for ruthlessness and for aiming for an adversary's jugular
vein in every dispute. He eventually earned a *Wall Street Journal*
headline: "Nixon Hatchet Man: Call It What You Will, Chuck Colson Handles President's Dirty Work."[4]

The ever-growing protest movements of the early 1970s, especially those aimed at the Nixon administration's war policies in
Southeast Asia, resulted in an atmosphere of paranoia in the White
House. When Daniel Ellsberg, a onetime member of Henry Kiss-
inger's staff, leaked to the media classified foreign policy information that became known as "the Pentagon Papers," White House
attempts to stop publication of the papers failed. At this juncture,
a group dubbed "the Plumbers" was formed to plug up such leaks.
Sent forth by Colson and headed by G. Gordon Liddy and E. Howard Hunt, they burglarized the office of Ellsberg's psychiatrist, seeking any kind of negative information to discredit him. The same
intensive paranoia affected the 1972 presidential campaign. At first
Colson denied the quip attributed to him, that he would run over
his own grandmother to ensure Nixon another four years. Then,
beginning to bask in his growing reputation as a hatchet man, he
got carried away and, in a memo, told his staff: "Many erroneous
things about me have found their way into print—but last week's
U. P. I. story that I would walk over my grandmother if necessary
is absolutely accurate."[5]

There was a delayed public reaction after the Watergate break-
in at Democratic campaign headquarters was revealed to be White
House-inspired. The matter did not affect the election, which was
a landslide victory for Nixon. Only during the next year, like storm
clouds gathering ever more ominously, did this single crime grow
in import in the consciousness of Americans. Fallout from the
incident eventually led to the resignation of Nixon and criminal
prosecutions which led to the jailing of twenty-seven men, Colson
one of them.

4. Colson, *Born Again*, 57.

5. Colson, *Born Again*, 71.

As he sat in the US Attorney's office waiting to appear before prosecutors, he felt a sense of shock. He wrote:

"As a lawyer I'd often been in the high-ceiling austere court-rooms, the warmly furnished judges' chambers, the handsome lawyers' libraries, lined with neat rows of books and portraits of judicial greats—where the eloquent arguments are made over abstract principles. For the first time I was inside the drab quarters of the army of marshals, clerks, and investigators who enforce the law where the law touches lives. I was beginning to sense how it felt to be personally caught in the cumbersome machinery."[6]

So short a time before one of the most powerful men in the world, able to act with seeming impunity, Colson now experienced what he called a "breakdown of power." Only in time would he realize such a breakdown was an offered moment of grace by which "God can break us to remake us."[7] A business friend, Tom Phillips contacted Colson at this moment and courageously shared with him that he himself had found inner peace in a conscious faith in Christ; in a real, not just lip-service, acceptance of Jesus into his life. Grasping at straws, Colson went to visit the man in his home. Phillips read to him from C. S. Lewis's *Mere Christianity*, and Lewis's words cut like a knife.

"As long as you are proud," Lewis wrote, "you cannot know God at all. A proud man is always looking down on things and people; and, of course, as long as you are looking down, you cannot see something that is above you."[8]

Colson remembered, "Suddenly I felt naked and unclean, my bravado defenses gone. I was exposed, unprotected, for Lewis's words were describing me."[9] He took the book and read it. He had been raised an Episcopalian, and his second wife was Catholic. But to his own shock, "in the ten years we'd been married, I realized, we'd never discussed God."[10] He began to pore

6. Colson, *Born Again*, 101.

7. Colson, *Loving God*, 169–70.

8. Colson, *Loving God*, 170.

9. Colson, *Born Again*, 112–13.

10. Colson, *Born Again*, 123.

through the Scriptures, wrestling with what he had accepted all his life unconsciously and glibly. "The words—both exciting and disturbing—pounded at me: Jesus Christ—lunatic or God? . . . If he is not God, He is nothing, least of all a great moral teacher. For what he taught includes the assertion that he is indeed God. I could not, I saw, take him on a slightly lower plateau because it is easier to do so, less troublesome to my intellect, less demanding of my faith, less challenging to my life. That would be substituting my mind for His, using Christianity where it helped to buttress my own notions, ignoring it where it didn't."[11]

It is a great confrontation with self for a person who has been a nominal Christian throughout life to make, for the first time as an adult, an intellectual assent that Jesus is God. It is another great confrontation with self for that person to share such a newfound faith with others—even though this is supposedly what Christians of every denomination do each time they gather in church. On the first occasion when Colson was called to do so among a small group of people in a living room, he thought:

"Are they going to think I'm some kind of nut? Do people really go around talking about their personal encounters with God?"

Overwhelmed with embarrassment, he finally murmured, "As a new Christian I have everything to learn. I know that. I'm grateful for any help you can give me."[12]

A decade later, writing about Colson's conversion, the news media would still insist on saying it was "convenient," coming as it did midway through the Watergate prosecutions. Quite to the contrary given his public position, his reputation for cynicism, and the expectation that he would be capable of doing anything to avoid conviction, his public profession of faith made him an immediate butt of ridicule. The political cartoonists had a field day. John Fischetti pictured him as a fake angel, held up by stage wiring over the White House roof, singing, "Coming for to Carry Me Home." Jeff MacNelly drew a fat barefoot friar seen from behind, having just passed a startled Nixon, who exclaims: "Colson?! . . ." Patrick

11. Colson, *Born Again*, 121.

12. Colson, *Born Again*, 150.

Oliphant portrayed him as a smug, Bible-toting, long-robed cleric carrying a sign which proclaimed: "Repent for lo, I am about to lay it on the House Judiciary Committee."[13]

Art Buchwald contributed a hilarious and scathing column in which a repentant Colson visits his still-suspicious grandmother to tell her that he has gotten religion, announcing: "It's true Granny, I'm no longer the mean, dirty rotten, unscrupulous trickster you used to bounce on your knee. I've been reborn, Granny." She refuses to open her door until he throws his car keys on the stoop and is then unable to kneel to pray with him because her knees were ruined the last time he ran her over.[14]

Dan Rather, hearing that Colson had joined in a prayer gathering at the White House, asked at a press conference, "Isn't someone around here worried at least about the symbolism of this?"[15]

Colson made the mistake of entering into Mike Wallace's arena on CBS's *60 Minutes*. It was a mistake, because Wallace relentlessly used Colson's conversion experience as a reason for public confession and demanded a full confession from his guest while the whole matter was still in court. When Colson backed away from this questioning, Wallace leaned back to sit in judgment, saying, "Let me understand something about this new Christianity then. You say that you are a new man in Jesus Christ. It seems as though your prior faith takes precedence over your new faith . . . Well, I confess you leave me somewhat bewildered, then, as to the meaning of your faith."[16] Wallace's jaded opinion was echoed in that of the American public. One man wrote to the *Philadelphia Enquirer*, saying of Colson, "I find it impossible to believe that he has accepted the spirit of goodness in any form while still he holds the knowledge of crimes in his heart and remains unwilling to let the truth come to light. Until he does that, he's no more than a pious

13. Colson, *Born Again*, 206.

14. Colson, *Born Again*, 189–90.

15. Colson, *Born Again*, 164.

16. Colson, *Born Again*, 218.

hypocrite, braying his prayers in public for no one's good but his own—he hopes they'll save his skin."[17]

On June 21, 1974, after pleading guilty to obstruction of justice, Colson was given a sentence of one to three years. Outside the courtroom he told reporters:

"What happened in court today was the court's will and the Lord's will. I have committed my life to Jesus Christ and I can work for him in prison as well as out."[18]

As noble as these words sounded, they had yet to be tested by the crucible of experience. He had hoped that life in military barracks would have prepared him for prison life, but he quickly found that, despite any superficial similarities, "there are sharper differences. In prison the man you befriend may steal your clean socks. Inmates seldom relax their guard even with those they know well. The sole aim in prison is to survive, make time pass, avoid trouble and get out."[19]

To his surprise he found that even visits became a negative factor in prison:

"Some prisoners actually preferred not to have visits from family and friends, not wanting to be seen in the dreary garb and surroundings of prison. Others believed that time passed faster without the emotional drain on them of the anticipation, the break in routine, and then the trauma of having to see loved ones depart. But for most prisoners the obstacle was economic: their families simply couldn't afford the cost of travel."[20]

He keenly felt the atmosphere of potential violence:

"Everything in the prison, including most of the men's nerves, seemed to be gripped in the same tense vise. It took little to unleash frayed nerves into swinging fists. A large number of men, even in places like Maxwell [Prison], have records of violence. Most fights are over such things as the program to be watched on television, the distance between bunks since space is such a

17. Colson, *Born Again*, 200.
18. Colson, *Born Again*, 250.
19. Colson, *Born Again*, 278.
20. Colson, *Born Again*, 280.

precious commodity, even the slamming of a locker door while another man is trying to sleep. Fights occur over petty thievery. I once listened to a huge, strapping convict shriek that he would 'kill' the man who had stolen soap from his locker."[21]

On one occasion Colson attempted to break up a fight between two inmates, and then shrank in terror when they both turned on him. He mollified them by lying that he had intervened because he had seen an officer come into view. Later, he tortured himself over his use of a lie to save his skin, something which seemed to spring too readily from the "old Colson." The onetime powerful White House aide was now leveled by common experience to sharing life with people who were powerless.[22]

One man in his section, a filling station manager, was doing time for cashing a customer's eighty-four-dollar check which turned out to have been stolen. It was a first offense. Colson observed, "His harsh sentence was the result of some ambitious prosecutor making a name for himself and a judge with a mean streak and a reputation for impulsiveness."[23]

Another man, a small-town bank president, was doing three years for a three-thousand-dollar tax fraud. "He was the first flesh-and-blood casualty I met of the great economic wars I had fought. Maybe, I thought, he ran afoul of one of those quirks or loopholes I'd engineered in the Internal Revenue laws. Prison was full of people prosecuted under laws I had written or enforced."

He at first brushed off the story of a doleful-eyed youngster who claimed he did not know the length of his sentence. Only in time did he realize that the boy was telling the truth. His case had been rushed through by a court-appointed attorney taking the lottery assignment Colson had once found so irksome himself. He had been marched before a judge who had mumbled inaudibly, cracked the gavel, and sent him off to jail. Any reader who thinks Colson is exaggerating here is heartily invited to take the time to sit in a courtroom of any good-sized municipality on any given day.

---

21. Colson, *Born Again*, 286.
22. Colson, *Born Again*, 286.
23. Colson, *Born Again*, 283–84.

Of his fellow inmates Colson wrote, "Most of those in prison with me were poor; or if they had money, it had been wiped out by their enormous trial costs."[24]

The newly realized Christian began to meet with prisoners who shared faith. They prayed together and gave comfort to one another. More and more he began to feel that God was educating him to some great purpose: "No one could understand this without being part of it, feeling the anxieties, knowing the helplessness, living in desolation. On a tiny scale it was the lesson of Jesus coming to us . . . For the rest of my life I would know and feel what it is like to be imprisoned, the steady gradual corrosion of a man's soul, like radiation slowly burning away tissue. Just as God in the person of Christ was not ashamed to call us his brothers, so it was that I should not be ashamed to call each of these fellow inmates my brothers. Furthermore, I was to love each one of them. And would I if I had not been there? Never, I admitted to myself."[25]

In 1976, shortly after his release, Colson established an organization which he called Prison Fellowship. He took to visiting some fifty prisons a year encouraging inmates to have faith in God and in themselves. He painted no rosy "post-born again" picture, emphasizing instead a need for self-direction and self-help. "The public doesn't care about you," he would insist to them, "They'd just as soon see you hang. What will change this place is . . . inmates who are daring to live as Christians."[26]

He avoided the extremes of many "born again" evangelists who preach a self-oriented "me and Jesus" salvation and avoided as well any narrow Pharisaical morality.

"We don't care about drinking and smoking and other petty legalisms," he declared. "We want genuine spiritual growth."[27]

Colson preached to prisoners that for true Christian conversion it is necessary to have both faith in Jesus and a change in the way one looks at one's fellow humans. He suggests as an acid test of

---

24. Colson, *Loving God*, 171.

25. Colson, *Born Again*, 283–84.

26. Colson, *Born Again*, 283–84.

27. Woodward and Monroe, "Colson Goes Back to Jail," 41.

goodwill that his listeners should be willing to pray for their wardens. Noting that he had made this a test for himself while a prisoner, he would add: "Sometimes I prayed he would be transferred."[28]

One of Colson's ongoing tasks as a White House power was to deal with lobbying clergy who loved to share limelight with politicians in power. He had come to see churches as just "another special interest group to hook into the political apparatus."[29] From the other side of the fence, he would warn all churches to avoid waltzing with politicians in much the same way that one would warn young people to avoid drugs.

While he avoided the bureaucratic tendencies of major denominations he equally avoided the instant salvation approach offered by television evangelists:

"Most of your American evangelical literature tends to be puffy, health-and-wealth-and-success kind of gospel" he observed, "You can call on God, and he will give you two cars in the garage and vacations and a permanent frozen smile, which to me is just cheap, phony, self-seeking Christianity."[30]

In his own writings Colson is catholic in an inclusive sense, seeing the Holy Spirit working in all denominations. In *Loving God*, a book of inspirational biographies, he mixes accounts of anti-slavery nineteenth-century Protestant ministers along with stories about nuns who run halfway houses. On the same page he quotes John Calvin and Pope Leo XIII to exemplify Christian belief that the Bible is the actual word of God. In the preface to his autobiographical book *Born Again* he suggests that many readers might think of the title as being an "overworked Protestant cliche." He tells how he came upon it:

"While accompanying my wife at her Roman Catholic Church one Sunday, Patty flipped open the hymnal, smiled and nudged me. We both knew at a moment that after long weeks of

28. "Breaching Church-State at Taconic."

29. Colson, *Born Again*, 109.

30. Fields, "PW Interviews," 118.

searching and rejecting hundreds of ideas, the title was on that page; the hymn was *Born Again*."[31]

If Colson felt that the desire of clergy to waltz with politicians "invites the seduction of the church," it does not mean that he felt Christians should be silent about political issues. The onetime seducer on behalf of the White House now played a strong adversarial role with regards America's criminal justice system.

Newsweek, noting that prison officials are cynical about the intrusion of Colson's Prison Fellowship, notes as well that "combative as ever, Colson is equally cynical about prison officials. 'Our problems are seldom with the inmates,' he says, 'the biggest problem we have is with prison staffs.' He stands in constant opposition to any push to build new prisons in the United States, claiming that this 'would only perpetuate an inhumane and useless system.'[32] The principle idea in Colson's vision of reform of the system is to separate truly dangerous criminals from those who are dangerous only in a legal sense. Instead of a knee-jerk, one-solution punishment of incarceration being meted out for every crime worthy of punishment, Colson would expand the use of sentences such as restitution, community service, and electronically surveyed house arrest. This would at least alleviate the present nightmare in which prisons become 'pits of violence and horror' where first time, youthful offenders are mixed with hardened criminals."[33]

William Buckley's conservative *National Review* endorsed Colson's efforts, saying, "we are already in his debt for the Prison Fellowship. The whole country would be indebted to him if his reforms were effected."[34] Two years after this the same publication noted the irony of government-paid corrections officers standing about to enable congregated inmates to hear the gospel preached and wondered if government officials who now have the power Colson once wielded might attack him for using the penal system

31. Colson, *Born Again*, 11.
32. Woodward and Monroe, "Colson Goes Back to Jail," 41.
33. Woodward and Monroe, "Colson Goes Back to Jail," 41.
34. "Prison Reform."

to proselytize, thus breaking the constitutional barrier between church and state.

"Will someone one day hand Charles Colson a summons for engaging in unlawful activity?" the magazine posed, "If so, the reenactment of the events in Jerusalem two thousand years ago becomes nearly letter perfect."[35]

The statement is an obvious journalistic hyperbole. Nevertheless, it is no exaggeration to point out that born-again preacher Charles Colson, onetime White House hatchet man, onetime prisoner, has done much to make the kingdom of God a reality in this present age.

---

35. "Breaching Church-State at Taconic," *National Review*, 10/10/84, 63.

Chapter 12

The Bible

"I Was in Prison . . ."

THROUGHOUT THE SCRIPTURES PRISONS are depicted as a fact of life; a place where one could find oneself not only because of wrongdoing but because of poverty or some fluke of bad fortune. Individuals, both good and bad, are thrown into prison, and oftentimes the good and the bad interact in ways that emphasize the chance and irony involved in incarceration.

Prophecy as a Capital Offense

As the Babylonians laid siege to Jerusalem in the sixth century BC, King Zedekiah reacted against the predictions of defeat made by Jeremiah and threw the prophet into prison.

As one reads the book of Jeremiah one gets the impression that the prophet was repeatedly in and out of prison and held in varying degrees of confinement depending on the state of war and the gravity of his prophecies. Thus, describing an early stage of the prophet's pronouncements, the author of the book explains to the reader: "At this time Jeremiah had not yet been put into prison" (Jer 37:4). This is soon amended; the prophet is described as locked in a "vaulted dungeon where he remained a long time" (Jer 37:16).

His enemies, hoping to kill him, had him taken from prison and thrown into a mud filled cistern. Ebed-melech, a devout Jewish Cushite (Ethiopian), intervened with King Zedekiah on the prophet's behalf. With permission, he took rag cloths from the palace and compassionately threw them down into the cistern so that Jeremiah could put them between the ropes and his armpits as he was pulled out, reducing any chafing pain. He was returned to the king's prison, where he remained "till the day Jerusalem was taken" (Jer 38:28).

The irony in the conclusion of this episode is that as Jeremiah was freed from prison, the invading army captured King Zedekiah. The king's sons were killed in front of him and then the king's eyes were gouged out, the last sight he ever saw being the death of his sons. Dragged to Babylon by the conquering army, the onetime royal persecutor of Jeremiah was himself "kept in prison until the day of his death" (Jer 52:11).

Until You've Paid the Last Penny

In the Sermon on the Mount, Jesus admonishes his followers to make peace on the way to court, "otherwise your opponent will hand you over to the judge, and the judge will hand you over to the guard, and you will be thrown into prison. Amen, I say to you, you will not be released until you have paid the last penny" (Matt 5:25–26). As a child I would hear that passage in church and be amazed at how stupid ancient society was to expect to get money from someone who was in jail and thus unable to earn the money to give the jailer. And then I grew up and began to work in jails and prisons where modern-day courts often incarcerate people for the same sorts of reasons; failure to pay support payments, compulsive gambling, and inability to keep personal finances straight, this sometimes ending up with embezzlement in a work situation ("I'm not stealing this; I'll slip it back in the till next week").

This practice would make sense if judges were dealing with wealthy individuals who have substantial amounts of money in their pockets. A garnishment of the person's wages would make sense. As it is these persons lose their source of income altogether and further payment becomes a matter of getting blood from a stone. But at least it is good to see that the Bible is still bull's-eye on target in the examples it uses.

Bread and Water

Other Biblical passages remind us of similarities between ancient and modern punishments behind bars. King Ahab was no better at receiving bad news than was Zedekiah. "I hate him," Ahab said of the prophet Micaiah, "because he prophesies not good but evil about me" (1 Kgs 22:8). Micaiah, seeing the people of Israel in the same pitiable way that would so deeply move Jesus, angered the king by describing them as being "like sheep without a shepherd" (1 Kgs 22:17). For voicing this insight, Micaiah was thrown into prison, the king ordering for him fare that would ever after be used to describe punishment diet: "Feed him scanty rations of bread and water."

In the Book of Judges we are given a glimpse of prison industry, which, every few generations, some theorists imagine that they are inventing anew—the delusion that one instills a sense of work ethic by assigning inmates to mindless, menial tasks. Sampson, weakened by the deceitful Delilah, who cut his strength-giving hair, and blinded by his Philistine captors, is put to work in prison, grinding at a mill (Judg 16:21). He does this long enough for his hair, and strength, to grow again, to the downfall of his jailers.

Joseph and His Coat of Prison Drabs

In the Book of Genesis, Joseph, the son of Jacob, sold into slavery by his own brothers, rises to a position of responsibility in the house of his Egyptian master Potiphar. The man's wife attempts to seduce Joseph, and when she fails to do so cries out that he has tried to rape her. Joseph is thrown into prison. What then becomes particularly notable in the ancient depiction of prison that follows is the similarity of its internal social structure as compared with that found in modern jails. The public does not like to hear it, but, as is often pointed out after a prison riot, prisons are run effectively only with the consent of the imprisoned.

In the Book of Genesis, depicting prison life millennia in the past, we are told of Joseph that the Lord caused the guards to be "well disposed toward him." Because of this, "the chief jailer put Joseph in charge of all the prisoners in the jail, and everything that had to be done there was done under his management" (Gen 39:22).

Unless one is in a facility where the officers in charge outnumber inmates several to one, a sort of tacit agreement is made. Everyone agrees that a microcosm of a larger society exists. Inmates have to move from one place to another and in situations where they outnumber officers. Given the need for everyday life, it is expected that the average inmate will accept the fact that the best must be made of a situation of incarceration and that the less fuss that happens is better for everybody involved, starting with oneself. The inmates agree to be ruled.

Officers, on the other hand, need help in running a facility, especially in taking care of menial tasks. They watch inmates carefully over a period of time and choose individuals to be "runners" on tiers (cleaning walkways, etc.) and "trustees" (working various jobs within the facility). On an every day basis a good relationship can develop between a tier officer and a runner. It is not unusual to come onto a tier and see two individuals, corrections officer and an inmate, playing chess at the tier desk. It fits into a category that might be labeled "living life with other human beings."

There is another aspect of prison life that has not changed since the time of Genesis. When movers and shakers of society come to jail, especially if they still have political connections and most especially if they still have access to money to put in other inmate's commissary accounts or in officials' pockets, they remain power brokers behind bars. Thus, in the story of Joseph, the royal cupbearer and royal baker to the pharaoh end up doing time. They retain their social clout in the society of prison, where Joseph, who is only a Hebrew slave, is assigned to be their servant. The young man accurately predicts the meaning of dreams which these men have, and Joseph's rise to power continues.

In all of this the author of Genesis never moralizes about the reality of prison. It is a fact of life. The one person who deservedly feels a sense of guilt about anything that transpires is the royal cup-bearer. Joseph, when he had interpreted the man's dream, asked him to intercede on his behalf. Given his freedom as Joseph had predicted would happen, the man went back to his life and never gave Joseph another thought. A full two years passed while Joseph remained in prison, and only when the pharaoh experienced a disturbing dream as had the cupbearer did the man guiltily think, "I am reminded of my negligence" (Gen 41:9). Two full years of thoughtlessness while another person suffered out of sight and thus out of mind.

End of the Line for the Greatest Human Born of Woman

Languishing in a prison cell ate away the strength of John the Baptist—the cousin of Jesus. No longer the firebrand we see in the first pages of the gospel story, he sends his messengers to Jesus pleading with him whether he is the one to come or if the people should seek another. Jesus sends consolation to him in the words of Isaiah depicting the work of the Messiah: that the blind would see, the lame walk, the deaf hear, the dead raised and the poor have the good news preached to them. One wonders if the discouraged Baptist, receiving this message, thought to ask why Jesus omitted a phrase from the same passage of Isaiah which he had included only shortly before when quoting the passage in the synagogue at Nazareth: "He has sent me to proclaim liberty to captives" (Luke 4:18). Instead, in its place Jesus adds, "blessed is the one who takes no offense at me" (Luke 7:23).

Jesus praises John at this moment of weakness as being the greatest human born of woman. What casual observers of the scene would have realized that the greatest human yet born was behind bars or that the greatest human yet born was executed because of a misuse of governmental authority and a request of an adolescent girl.

Saul (aka Paul)

For those who take for granted the reality of life in the Holy Spirit, prisons can serve as an element in a purification process, and no one came to see this more clearly than Paul of Tarsus. It is of note that when he writes from a jail cell he describes himself as a "prisoner of Christ." Not a prisoner because of Christ, but of Christ. Paul thus heightens the earthly fact of incarceration into a purification process, a mystical union with God's plan.

He never forgot and would often speak out as to how before his own conversion "I persecuted this way to death, binding both men and women and delivering them to prison" (Acts 22:4). Moreover, he had been guilty of the martyrdom of "many of the Holy ones . . . When they were to be put to death I cast my vote against them" (Acts 26:10). Paul of Tarsus was never under any illusions about himself. Owing above all to his active role in the mob killing of Stephen the deacon, he could assert, "I am the least of the apostles; in fact, because I persecuted the church of God, I do not even deserve the name" (1 Cor 15:11).

The infant Christian community at first agreed with him. When he returned to Jerusalem after his conversion on the road to Damascus they warily held back from him and "even refused to believe that he was a disciple" (Acts 9:26–29). Were it not for the willingness of Barnabas to believe in the conversion of a murderer, Paul of Tarsus might have lived his life in the desert as an unheard-of Christian hermit and been lost to history. Barnabas would not accept the community's rejection of the criminal Saul, saying it was a denial of everything Jesus lived and taught. He took him in tow, bringing him to the apostles and insisting that they take his conversion at face value.

Paul the Jailhouse Preacher

In the middle of the Acts of the Apostles Paul is thrown into jail at Philippi. Put in a special security holding area, he and his missionary companion Silas are preaching and singing hymns at midnight when an earthquake undoes both chains and doors.

The jailer panics, thinking that all his prisoners have escaped. Paul assures him that everyone is still there. Abashed, the man brings the two Christians into his home and dresses the wounds they had received in a beating. Paul manages to convert the whole household. Then, in typical Paul manner, he refuses to quietly leave Philippi when the authorities realize that they have illegally jailed a Roman citizen. Paul insists that these authorities publicly and officially release him. He knew how to make the most of publicity, and he was out to convert the world. The physical fact of prison was a detail that did not exclude anyone involved from hearing the good news; no good guys or bad guys, them or us, prisoners or keepers. Everyone had to be saved.

During the decades of time that Paul traveled about the Mediterranean world preaching faith in Jesus there were numerous occasions when he would be incarcerated for short periods of time. This was providential for the infant Christian community and for the history of early Christianity. It was when he was in jail that activist Paul generally sat down long enough to compose the letters that would become the New Testament Epistles. The last chapters of the Acts of the Apostles chronicles that Paul was arrested in Jerusalem and kept for a long time as a prisoner there, perhaps occupying at first the same cell in the Fortress Antonia where Jesus was kept before being executed.

Taken to Caesarea, Paul waited two full years for a court date there, and when eventually he was brought to Rome he spent another two years in house arrest. A prisoner of Christ, not the state, Paul never stopped converting, preaching to the soldiers, governors, local kings, whoever was in range of his voice or his pen. Jails were his pulpits.

"Dismas" the What?—Robber?—
Murderer?—Child Abuser?

Christians have concocted a mythic rap sheet for the sainted criminal who died on the cross next to Jesus, assured by Jesus that he would be that day with him in Paradise. We have given him the name (not in the Bible) of "Dismas," meaning "thief," have dubbed him the "good thief," and love to refer to him as "the thief who stole heaven." In doing so we show that we want to have our pieties mixed with our prejudices.

Nothing in the Bible intimates that the unnamed man was a thief. We've colored him as such so that we can make him into a sort of Robin Hood, an attractive matinee idol, vine-swinging, twinkle-in-the-eye bad guy; but not really a bad guy. The likeliest guess is that "Dismas" was a revolutionary. St. Mark tells us that Barabbas, the convict freed instead of Jesus, had been imprisoned "with the rebels who had committed murder in a rebellion" (Mark 15:7). If our Saint Dismas was one of them, he was capable of slitting a throat. However, the Greek word used in the gospel for "revolutionary" can also mean "robber." A robber is very different than a thief. A thief is someone who takes someone's property by stealth. Victims of theft generally do not know that they have been the victim of a theft until it is over and done with. A robber confronts a victim face-to-face and demands something, threatening to take limb or life along with the demanded property. A robber is a violent person.

Hanging on the cross, Saint Dismas acknowledged the depth of his criminality by saying to the third man being crucified, "We have been condemned justly, for the sentence we received corresponds to our crimes" (Luke 24:41). He was guilty of something which he himself thought fit a death sentence. I would suggest that it would be far more fitting to the scene as it is written to let our imaginations run not in a direction that would sugarcoat the story and thus reduce the demand it places upon our forgiveness but in a direction that imagines a crime that we too might think fitting of a death sentence. Think despicable. Think mass murder. Think child abuser. Think rape. Then fill in the time honored pious gush: "St. Dismas, the good _____ who stole heaven." It doesn't work as well for us, does it? But it works well to describe the forgiveness of which Jesus spoke.

Our Convict God

In Matthew 25:36 Jesus demands that we visit those in prison, making it a condition of our own acceptance into heaven. He does not in any way distinguish, or allow us to distinguish, between good or bad, between worthy or unworthy, prisoners. The faces of the very least of them (including the lowest in terms of self-degradation) must be seen as the face of Christ. In his humanness Christ "earned" the right to demand this of us. He died in the company of "convicts"—those who are legally "convicted" of crime. He was one of them.

There are two places in Jerusalem that have ancient jail cells that may well be cells where Jesus was kept while he was awaiting trial and then his execution. The first place is a recently exhumed building that was once the house of Caiaphas the high priest. It has a dungeon cell in an underground area beneath the main rooms of the building. If Jesus were held for any time in this place while the Sanhedrin debated about what to do with him, he had to be rope-lowered into and rope-pulled out of this place through a hole in the floor in the same way that the prophet Jeremiah was lowered into the cistern which served as a dungeon for him five centuries earlier.

The second site is in a remnant section of the Roman garrison's Fortress Antonia. The section contains a holding area cell in which Jesus would probably have been kept while the empire's governor decided how to be rid of him. One can go inside the cell and pull the barred gate shut. Two considerations had a profound impact upon me when I did so. The lesser impact was that little has changed about jail cells in two thousand years of time. A stone and metal cage for humans remains a stone and metal cage for humans. The more profound consideration is to realize that one is standing in the human-made cage which imprisoned the Lord of all creation. As so in history he was branded, scarred with nail holes in hands and feet; a lance mark piercing his side, his heart; scars for all eternity, even in his glory. Our scars, taken upon himself, will bring us to share in his eternal glory if we turn to him.

Recently at a jail where I minister we received from the Immaculate Heart of Mary Learning Center a striking photo sent as a handout to be given to inmates. It is a silhouette photo depiction of Jesus, in a cell, his thorn-crowned head bowed. He is leaning against and holding on to the bars of the cell with one hand. It is a body posture I have seen countless times in the past decades; a posture of pain, of appeal—perhaps for justice—perhaps for mercy—perhaps just to be fairly and equably heard in court. Underneath the picture is written: "Know that I am always with you—Your Savior, Jesus."

Even the ancient world kept the record of crimes committed by an individual that we refer to as a "rap sheet." The Roman Governor Pontius Pilate, in three languages—Hebrew, Greek, and Latin—nailed to the cross of Jesus a "rap sheet" stating the only charge for which he was executed. Pilate waved off the protests of the temple priests as they complained, "Put that he said he was . . ." Pilate told the priests, "What I have written I have written." He had written, "This is Jesus, King of the Jews" (Matt 27:35–37).

Little wonder that, even on a level of human emotion, Jesus could commiserate so totally to his fellow convicted criminals. Dismas, one of the rare few people in the Gospels who addresses Jesus by his name, asked, "Jesus, remember me when you come in to your kingdom." Jesus assured him, "This very day you will be in paradise" (Luke 24:33–43).

I sometimes wonder if this "thief who stole heaven" might have been like so many young con artists one meets while walking the intake tiers of a jail or prison, who jumps up from his cot and says something like, "Oh, I was hoping to see a chaplain" in a tone that says, "What's to lose?" I'm fine with it. It's part of the turf.

At the other extreme one encounters sad individuals like the other convict crucified with Jesus, who say something like, "You've got nothing to give me; get out of my face." One can see in him—or her—the child who was abused and neglected in many ways from early childhood, shoved from one semi-caretaker situation to another—who has never known constant love or affirmation; who took to the streets; and who, when turning sixteen, the age at which in most states he or she can be put in adult jails, is still an adolescent but can legally be called an adult.

Maybe the embittered man (or sixteen-year-old) on the third cross on Calvary is saying, "You've got nothing to give me."

Many people presume that Dismas goes to heaven and the criminal on the third cross was not "saved." The Gospels do not say that. We say that. Jesus, as he is dying, asks his heavenly Father to forgive those who nailed him to the cross. Would he not include the poor man crucified with him? To not do so would be totally unlike Jesus, who came to us as our Savior. I believe that when Dismas awakened in paradise, Jesus greeted him. I also believe with all my heart that when the embittered fellow convict of Jesus awakened in Paradise, Jesus said to him, "Welcome home."

Bibliography

"Alessandro Serenelli." Wikipedia. https://en.wikipedia.org/wiki/Alessandro_Serenelli.

"Alessandro Serenelli Letter." Universe of Faith, Oct 28, 2016. https://universeoffaith.org/alessandro-serenelli-letter/.

Anonymous. "A Prisoner's Tribute." *Star of Hope*, July 15, 1900.

Baldwin, Anne. *Catherine of Siena: A Biography*. Huntington, IN: Our Sunday Visitor, 1987.

Baus, Karl. "From the Apostolic Community to Constantinople." In *Handbook of Church History*, 435–504. New York: Herder & Herder, 1965.

Bosco, John. *Saint Joseph Cafasso: Priest of the Gallows*. Gastonia, NC: Tan, 1983.

"Breaching Church and State at Taconic." *National Review*, May 14, 1982, page 63.

Catherine of Siena. *I, Catherine: Selected Writings*. Glasgow: William Collins, 1851.

Colson, Charles. *Born Again*. Old Tappen, NJ: Chosen Books, 1976.

———. *Loving God*. Grand Rapids: Zondervan, 1997.

Cook, Stanley A., et al., eds. *The Imperial Crisis and Recovery, A.D. 193–324*. The Cambridge Ancient History 12. Cambridge: Cambridge University Press, 1956.

Day, Dorothy. *The Long Loneliness*. New York: Harper, 1952.

———. *Therese*. Notre Dame, IN: Notre Dame University Press, 1960.

de La Bedoyere, Michael. *Catherine, Saint of Siena*. London: Hollis and Carter, 1947.

Bibliography

———. *The Life of Catherine Benincasa: Catherine, Saint of Siena*. London: Hollis and Carter, 1947.

Delaney, John J. *The Dictionary of Saints*. New York: Doubleday, 1980.

Di Donato, Pietro. *The Penitent*. New York: Popular Library, 1962.

Dollinger, John J. von. *Hippolytus and Callistus: The Church of Rome in the First Half of the Third Century*. Edinburgh: Hollis and Carter, 1876.

Duchesne, Louis. *Early History of the Christian Church: From Its Foundation to the End of the Fifth Century*. Harlow, UK: Longmans, Green & Co., 1912.

Ellman, Richard. *Oscar Wilde*. New York: Alfred A. Knopf, 1982.

Faupel, John F. *African Holocaust*. New York: P. J. Kenedy & Sons, 1962.

Fields, Howard. "PW Interviews." *Publishers Weekly*, September 10, 1983.

Flourney, Park Poindexter. *The Searchlight of St. Hippolytus: The Papacy and the New Testament in the Light of Discovery*. Whitefish, MT: Kessinger, 2010.

Francis of Assisi. *The Little Flowers*. Orleans, MA: Paraclete, 2016.

Frankel, Nicholas. *Oscar Wilde: The Unrepentant Years*. Cambridge, MA: Harvard University Press, 2018.

Gallagher, Ann Miriam. "Catherine Josephine Seton and the New York Mercy Experience." Washington. 1997.

Green, Julien. *God's Fool: The Life and Times of Francis of Assisi*. New York: HarperOne, 1985.

Holland, Merlin. *Complete Works of Oscar Wilde*. London: HarperCollins, 1994.

Hutchinson, R. A. *Diocesan Priest Saints*. St. Louis, MO: Herder & Herder, 1958.

Hyde, H. Montgomery. *Oscar Wilde*. New York: Farrar, Straus & Giroux, 1975.

Jalbert, Arthur. *Walk While You Have the Light*. St. Meinrad, IN: CreateSpace, 2011.

Jørgensen, Johannes. *Don Bosco*. London, 1934.

———. *Saint Catherine of Siena*. Translated by Ingeborg Lund. New York: Sheed & Ward, 1954.

Kelly, John Norman Davidson. *The Oxford Dictionary of Popes*. Oxford: Oxford University Press, 1986.

Klein, Peter, ed. "Peace Prayer of St. Francis." In *The Catholic Source Book*, 31. 3rd ed. Orlando: Brown-Roa, 2000.

McGuire, M. R. "St. Hyppolytus of Rome." *New Catholic Encyclopedia*, 6.1140. Washington, DC: 1967.

Miller, William D. *Dorothy Day: A Biography*. San Francisco: Harper & Row, 1982.

Mindszenty, József. *Memoirs*. New York: Macmillan, 1974.

"Mwanga II of Buganda." Wikipedia, last edited Oct 13, 2022. https://en.wikipedia.org/wiki/Mwanga_II_of_Buganda.

Phelan, Edna Beyer. *Don Bosco: A Spiritual Portrait*. Garden City, NY: Doubleday, 1963.

"Prison Reform." *National Review*, May 14, 1982.

Readers' Guide to Periodical Literature. H. W. Wilson Company. EBSCO Information Service. N.p.: Andesite Press, 2017.

Rohrbach, P. T. "Saint Therese of Lisieux." *New Catholic Encyclopedia*, 14.68. Washington, DC: 1967.

Bibliography

Sabatier, Paul. *Life of St. Francis of Assisi*. New York: Scribner's, 1894.

Shaw, Richard. *John Dubois: Founding Father*. Yonkers, NY: United States Catholic History Society, 1983.

Sturges, Matthew. *Oscar Wilde: A Life*. New York: Knopf Doubleday, 2012.

Therese of Lisieux. *Autobiography of a Soul*. Translated by Ronald Knox. New York: P. J. Kenedy and Sons, 1958.

Thomas of Celano. "The First Life of Saint Francis of Assisi." Edited by Marion Habig. In *The English Omnibus of the Sources for the Life of Saint Francis*. Chicago: Triangle Publishers, 1972.

———. "The Second Life of Saint Francis." Edited by Marion Habig. In *The English Omnibus of the Sources for the Life of Saint Francis*. Chicago: Triangle Publishers, 1972.

Tuchman, Barbara. *A Distant Mirror: The Calamitous Fourteenth Century*. New York: Random House, 1987.

Tucker, Jeffrey. "Oscar Wilde/Roman Catholic." *Crisis Magazine*, April 2001.

Wilde, Oscar. *The Complete Works of Oscar Wilde*. London: Harper Collins, 1948.

———. *The Letters of Oscar Wilde*. Edited by Rupert Davis. New York: Barnes & Noble, 1994.

———. *The Wit and Humor of Oscar Wilde*. Mineola, NY: Dover, 1959.

Woodward, Kenneth, and Sylvester Monroe. "Colson Goes Back to Jail." *Newsweek*, Sep 7, 1981.

Wordsworth, Christopher. *Saint Hippolytus and the Church of Rome in the Earlier Part of the Third Century*. London: Rivingtons, 1880.

Made in United States
North Haven, CT
25 March 2023

34537188R00075